A STUDY OF BOWS AND ARROWS

TRADITIONAL ARCHERY METHODS, EQUIPMENT CRAFTING, AND COMPARISON OF ANCIENT NATIVE AMERICAN BOWS

BY **SAXTON POPE**

ORIGINALLY PUBLISHED IN 1923

LEGACY EDITION

THE LIBRARY OF ANCIENT & TRADITIONAL ARCHERY
BOOK 2

FEATURING
REMASTERED CLASSIC WORKS OF THE HIGHEST QUALITY FROM **THE TIMELESS MASTERS AND TEACHERS** OF TRADITIONAL HANDCRAFTS AND OUTDOORS SKILLS

Doublebit Press
Eugene, OR

New content, introduction, and annotations
Copyright © 2020 by Doublebit Press. All rights reserved.

Doublebit Press is an imprint of Eagle Nest Press
www.doublebitpress.com | Eugene, OR, USA

Original content under the public domain. First published in 1923 by Saxton Pope.

This title, along with other Doublebit Press books are available at a volume discount for youth groups, outdoors clubs, craft groups, or reading groups. Contact us at info@doublebitpress.com for more information.

Doublebit Press Legacy Edition ISBNs
Hardcover: 978-1-64389-113-2
Paperback: 978-1-64389-114-9

Disclaimer: Because of its age and historic context, this text could contain content on present-day inappropriate outdoors activities, outdated medical information, unsafe chemical and mechanical processes, or culturally and racially insensitive content. Doublebit Press, or its employees, authors, and other affiliates, assume no liability for any actions performed by readers or any damages that might be related to information contained in this book. This text has been published for historical study and for personal literary enrichment toward the goal of the preservation of American outdoors history and heritage.

First Doublebit Press Legacy Edition Printing, 2020

Printed in the United States of America
when purchased at retail in the USA

INTRODUCTION
To The Doublebit Press Legacy Edition

The old experts of the woods, mountains, and farm country life taught timeless principles and skills for decades. Through their books, the old experts offered rich descriptions of the outdoor world and encouraged learning through personal experiences in nature. Over the last 125 years, handcrafts, artisanal works, outdoors activities, and our experiences with nature have substantially changed. Many things have gotten simpler as equipment and processes have improved, and life outside, on the farm, or on the trail now brings with it many of the same comforts enjoyed in town. In addition, some activities of the old days are now no longer in vogue, or are even outright considered inappropriate or illegal. However, despite many of the positive changes in handcrafting, traditional skills, and outdoors methods that have occurred over the years, *there are many other skills and much knowledge that are at risk of being lost* that should never be forgotten.

By publishing Legacy Editions of classic texts on handcrafts, artisanal skills, nature lore, survival, and outdoors and camping life, it is our goal at Doublebit Press to do what we can to preserve and share the works from forgotten teachers that form the cornerstone of the authentic and hard-wrought American tradition of self-sustainability and self-reliance. Through remastered reprint editions of timeless classics of traditional crafts, classic methods, and outdoor recreation, perhaps we can regain some of this lost knowledge for future generations.

On the frontier, folks made virtually everything by hand. Old farmers' knowledge and homestead skills were passed on to the future generation because it meant survival. In addition, much of traditional handcrafts and outdoors life knowledge was passed on from American Indians – the original handcrafters and outdoorsmen of the Americas.

Today, much of the handcrafted items of the frontier are made in factories, only briefly seeing a human during the process (if at all). Making things by hand indeed takes much (often strenuous) work, but it provides an extreme sense of pride in the finished job. Instantly, all hand-made items come with a story on their creation. Most importantly, though, making items with traditional methods gives you experience and knowledge of how things work.

This is similar to the case of camping and the modern outdoors experience, with neatly arranged campsites at public campgrounds and camping gear that has been meticulously improved and tested in both the lab and the field. These changes have also caused us to lose this traditional knowledge, having it buried in the latest high-tech iteration of your latest camp gadget.

Many modern conveniences are only a brief trek away, with many parks, campgrounds, and even forests having easy-access roads, convenience stores, and even cell phone signal. In some ways, it is much easier to camp and go outdoors today, and that is a good thing! We should not be miserable when we go outside — lovers of the outdoors know the essential restorative capability that the woods can have on the body, mind, and soul. But to experience it, you need to not be surrounded by modern high-tech robotic coffee pots, tents that build themselves, or watches that tell you how to do everything!

Although things have gotten easier on us in the 21st Century when it comes to handcrafts and the outdoors, it certainly does not mean that we should forget the foundations of technical skills, artisanal production, and outdoors lore. All of the modern tools and cool gizmos that make our lives easier are all founded on principles of traditional methods that the old masters knew well and taught to those who would listen. We just have to look deeply into the design of our modern gadgets and factories to see the original methods and traditional skills at play.

Every woods master and artisan had their own curriculum or thought some things were more important than others. The old masters also taught common things in slightly different ways or did things differently than others. That's what makes each of the experts different and worth reading. There's no universal way of doing something, especially today. Learning to go about something differently helps with mastery or learn a new skill altogether. Basically, you learn intimately how things work, giving you great skill with adapting and being flexible when the need arises.

Again, to use the metaphor from the above paragraphs, traditional skills mastery consists of learning the basic building blocks of how and why the old artisans made things, how they lived outdoors, and why woods and nature lore mattered. Everything is intertwined, and doing it by hand increases your knowledge of this complex network. Each master goes about describing these building blocks differently or shows a different aspect of them.

Therefore, we have decided to publish this Legacy Edition reprint in our collection of traditional handcraft and outdoors life classics. This book is an important contribution to the early American traditional skills and outdoors literature, and has important historical and collector value toward preserving the American tradition of self-sufficiency and artisan production. The knowledge it holds is an invaluable reference for practicing outdoors skills and hand craft methods. Its chapters thoroughly discuss some of the essential building blocks of knowledge that are fundamental but may have been forgotten as equipment gets fancier and technology gets smarter. In short, this book was chosen for Legacy Edition printing because much of the basic skills and knowledge it contains has been forgotten or put to the wayside in trade for more modern conveniences and methods.

Although the editors at Doublebit Press are thrilled to have comfortable experiences in the woods and love our modern equipment for making cool hand-made projects, we are also realizing that the basic skills taught by the old masters are more essential than ever as our culture becomes more and more hooked on digital stuff. We don't want to risk forgetting the important steps, skills, or building blocks involved with each step of traditional methods. Sometimes, *there's no substitute for just doing something on your own, by hand.* Sometimes, to truly learn something is to *just do it by hand.* The Legacy Edition series represents the essential contributions to the American handcraft and outdoors tradition by the great experts.

With technology playing a major role in everyday life, sometimes we need to take a step back in time to find those basic building blocks used for gaining mastery – the things that we have luckily not completely lost and has been recorded in books over the last two centuries. These skills aren't forgotten, they've just been shelved. *It's time to unshelve them once again and reclaim the lost knowledge of self-sufficiency.*

Based on this commitment to preserving our outdoors and handcraft heritage, we have taken great pride in publishing this book as a complete original work without any editorial changes or revisions. We hope it is worthy of both study and collection by handcrafters and outdoors folk in the modern era and to fulfill its status as a Legacy Edition by passing along to the libraries of future generations.

Unlike many other low-resolution photocopy reproductions of classic books that are common on the market, this Legacy Edition does not simply place poor photography of old texts on our pages and use error-prone optical scanning or computer-generated text. We want our work to speak for itself and reflect the quality demanded by our customers who spend their hard-earned money. With this in mind, each Legacy Edition book that has been chosen for publication is carefully remastered from original print books, *with the Doublebit Legacy Edition printed and laid out in the exact way that it was presented at its original publication.* Our Legacy Edition books are inspired by the original covers of first-edition texts, embracing the beauty that is in both the simplicity and sometimes ornate decoration of vintage and antique books. We want provide a beautiful, memorable experience that is as true to the original text as best as possible, but with the aid of modern technology to make as meaningful a reading experience as possible for books that are typically over a century old.

Because of its age and because it is presented in its original form, the book may contain misspellings, inking errors, and other print blemishes that were common for the age. However, these are exactly the things that we feel give the book its character, which we preserved in this Legacy Edition. During digitization, we did our best to ensure that each illustration in the text was clean and sharp with the least amount of loss from being copied and digitized as possible. Full-page plate illustrations are presented as they were found, often including the extra blank page that was often behind a plate and plate pagination. For the covers, we use the original cover design as our template to give the book its original feel. We are sure you'll appreciate the fine touches and attention to detail that your Legacy Edition has to offer.

For traditional handcrafters and outdoors enthusiasts who demand the best from their equipment, this Doublebit Press Legacy Edition reprint was made with you in mind. Both important and minor details have equally both been accounted for by our publishing staff, down to the cover, font, layout, and images. It is the goal of Doublebit Legacy Edition series to preserve America's handcrafting and outdoors heritage, but also be cherished as collectible pieces, worthy of collection in any person's library and that can be passed to future generations.

Every book selected to be in this series offers unique views and instruction on important skills, advice, tips, tidbits, anecdotes, stories, and experiences that will enrichen the repertoire of any person looking to learn the skills it contains. To learn the most basic building blocks leads to mastery of all its aspects.

Studying This Book
The pages within this book present an overwhelming amount of information, facts, and directions to memorize that are often outdated and at the least, out of practice by modern standards. That doesn't mean that these pages have nothing to teach! It's just going to likely be new stuff for many readers.

Our one suggestion is *don't try to memorize everything,* especially when you're thumbing through the book or even reading it cover-to-cover. Many of our Legacy Edition books are antique or vintage. These writings from the late 1800's to early 1900's can be dense and out of style for someone not used to reading these types of books. Instead, gain some basic familiarity with each topic by thumbing through the pages, looking at the illustrations, and seeing the section headers. Then, choose a few topics or skills for deeper study.

Before you start a crafting project, or before camping or other outdoors trips can even begin, some planning and reflection is useful. First, it might be helpful to read through the book with plans in mind. The book can provide useful material for close study and reflection before you acquire equipment or head out to the field to practice.

Secondly, once you've come up with a practice plan, you will of course want to start doing tasks and skills. Doublebit Legacy Edition reprints all represent *learning by doing*, with each book containing many skills to master that have long sense been out of practice. But this is exactly why we print these books – these skills and methods should not be forgotten!

Any of the old artisans and tutors of woodcraft will tell you in their classic books that you can only truly learn how do stuff by *actually doing it*. Home study indeed does you well by using the many guidebooks that have been published over the previous 125 years. However, hundreds more lessons will become immediately available to you the moment you start with some of the old-style tasks.

For instance, before the days of camping outfitters, outdoors adventurers made their gear, which was tailored to their individual needs. Many experiments were done in the field to tweak their gear to get that ever-changing point of "perfect." Aside from experiencing wonderful lessons in history, getting outside and doing some of the activities this book will give you an appreciation for modern advances in outdoors and handcraft method and tools of the trade, as well as a deeper understanding of the foundations of outdoors and hand-craft life in the event that your gear fails you or you otherwise find yourself in situations where knowing the principles will get you unstuck fast.

If we were to tally up each of the individual tips in the Doublebit Library of Legacy Edition reprints, they would easily number in the thousands. The old masters represent centuries of previous knowledge that have been all but lost to 21st Century, technology-driven folks. To this point, although experience and *actually doing stuff* are the best forms of learning, taking a mindful approach to study of these works also benefit your development as a competent outdoorsperson and handcrafter.

You may also find it invaluable to take these volumes with you on your camping or other outdoors trips. In addition to having reading material on a variety of topics in the field for down time, you'll also find a thousand things to try in these pages if you're bored. Although skills may be best studied when in the field through experience and reflection, you may also study woods skills at home as well. Gaining familiarity through reading, videos, and other media are a great start toward building your ability toward gaining mastery in the field.

A STUDY OF
BOWS AND ARROWS

BY

SAXTON T. POPE

UNIVERSITY OF CALIFORNIA PRESS
BERKELEY, CALIFORNIA

UNIVERSITY OF CALIFORNIA PRESS
BERKELEY, CALIFORNIA

CAMBRIDGE UNIVERSITY PRESS
LONDON, ENGLAND

PRINTED IN THE UNITED STATES OF AMERICA

CONTENTS

	PAGE
PRELIMINARY CONSIDERATIONS	3
Bows	3
Arrows	5
Flight shooting	6
Bows	8
Bows chiefly from the University of California	8
Jessop bows	16
Bows from the American Museum of Natural History	20
Tartar bows	23
Japanese bows	27
Negrito bow	28
Polynesian bow	29
Replicas of ancient bows	30
An experiment on bow strings	35
Experimental data on bow wood	36
Arrows	40
Penetration of arrows	40
Velocity of arrows	41
Striking force of arrows	42
Characteristic features of arrows	44
Experiments in rigidity of arrows	44
Arrow feathers	46
Experiment in arrow rotation	49
Different arrowheads and their penetration	50
Comparative penetration of steel and obsidian heads	55
Penetration of the bodkin point	56
Penetration of hunting arrows	58
The flight of aboriginal arrows	59
Comparison of arrows	60
Comparison of arrows and bullets	61
Conclusions	62
Explanations of plates	64

PLATES

		PAGE
Plate 1.	An old painting of St. Sebastian	65
Plate 2.	Bows used in the tests	67
Plate 3.	Bows used in the tests	69
Plate 4.	Bows and arrows from the Jessop collection	71
Plate 5.	American Museum of Natural History bows	73
Plate 6.	Tartar bows	75
Plate 7.	Japanese archer and bow	77
Plate 8.	Negrito, Cliff dweller, and Wintun bows and arrows	79
Plate 9.	Replicas of Turkish composite and English bows	81
Plate 10.	Arrows used in the tests	83
Plate 11.	Aboriginal arrows in the University Museum of Anthropology	85
Plate 12.	Various arrows	87
Plate 13.	Arrowheads used in penetration tests	89
Plate 14.	Ancient Syrian arrowheads	91
Plate 15.	Arrows penetrating a fir board	93
Plate 16.	Skull pierced through the orbit by an arrow	95
Plate 17.	Arrow shot through a coat of mail	97
Plate 18.	Penetration of arrows	99
Plate 19.	Penetration of arrows	101
Plate 20.	Penetration of obsidian in bone	103

A STUDY OF BOWS AND ARROWS

BY

SAXTON T. POPE

A contest of strength between peoples will always interest human beings; rivalry in the arms and implements of war is one of the fascinations of national competition. It is therefore a matter of interest both to the anthropologist and the practical archer to know what is the actual casting quality and strength of the best specimens of bows of different aboriginal tribes and nations of the world. And, as further incentive to this study, is the rapid disappearance of archery as civilization advances.

In the following experiments a detailed test of the shooting quality of a series of bows was undertaken, and with it certain correlated experiments concerning the penetration of arrows. Most of these bows were selected from hundreds in possession of the Museum of Anthropology of the University of California. They are the best preserved and strongest specimens in that large collection. In no instance is it apparent that age has led to deterioration in their strength. In fact, the greatest modern flight shot—four hundred and fifty-nine yards—has recently been made by Ingo Simon at La Tourque, France, with a Turkish composite bow reported to be nearly two hundred years old.[1] Age increases the brittleness, resiliency, and casting power of a wooden bow up to the point where fragility renders it unsafe to shoot. In all our tests we broke only two bows: a specimen from the Yukon, and an Osage Indian bow. To insure that no personal element of muscular weakness entered into the problem of the casting power of these weapons I had them shot by an old and experienced archer, Mr. W. J. Compton, a very powerful man and one accustomed to shoot the bow for more than thirty years. I also was able to draw the strongest of these bows, and myself checked up the results.

---

[1] Archers' Register, 1914.

PRELIMINARY CONSIDERATIONS

BOWS—

The *anatomy* of a bow: The length usually is measured from the two opposite points of attachment of the string or between nocks. The nocks are the depressions or notches which serve to hold the string from slipping. The space occupied by the hand in holding the bow is termed the handgrip or handle. The regions between the handgrip and the nocks are termed the limbs. The back of the bow is its convex side when strung. The concave side is called the belly. A bow which, when unstrung, reverses its curve, is called reflexed, while one which maintains a certain amount of curvature is said to follow the string. Setting the string tight on a bow is termed "bracing it."

The *capacity* of a bow to throw an arrow a given distance may be taken as a criterion of its value as a weapon, wherewith to do damage, either in the chase or in conflict. The weight and velocity of the missile are its chief characteristics, whether it be a stone, a bullet, or an arrow.

Besides the cast of a bow, there are other factors that bear directly upon its function, namely: material, size, strength, quality of recoil or action.

The *material* used in the construction of a bow is dictated, as a rule, by circumstances and environment. A great deal depends upon whether a bow is made of a simple wooden stave, a combination of wood and bone, or of wood, horn, sinew, and glue. All of these react differently to heat and moisture: an elaborate composite bow would quickly lose its utility in a damp climate; a simple wooden stave also becomes flaccid in extremely hot weather.

Size.—On horseback, or hunting in brushy country, a short bow is more convenient to use: Indian, Persian, and Turkish bows bear witness to this fact. The ancient English archer could use a longbow because he was a foot soldier.

The *strength* of a bow is determined by the strength of the man and the purpose of the weapon. Most American Indian bows now extant seem constructed entirely for hunting small game, and consequently do not demand great power. But in days gone by, the object of every archer was in time of war to deal as powerful a blow, at as great a distance, as possible.

Men of different nations do not differ greatly in strength. A bow may pull or "weigh" a great deal yet not have corresponding resiliency and lack a cast proportionate to its resistance. This would then be called a bow of dull cast, and one of active recoil and quick response would be called quick or lively, or brilliant in cast.

Because of lack of proper balance or distribution of action in the arc of a bow, it may recoil so unevenly as to jar the hand, or kick in the grasp, or be unpleasant to use. This sort of bow militates against accurate shooting and would be called a "harsh bow," while a bow well balanced and pleasant to shoot has been called soft, or a "sweet bow."

The amount of force necessary to draw a bow is called the *weight* of a bow. Apparently the Chinese were the first people to classify bows according to weight standards. The first reference to weights in England seems to date from the renaissance of archery, about

1798. The method of estimating the strength of a bow was either to suspend weights to the string until the arrow length was drawn, or to use a steelyard attached to the string while full drawn. By fixing the bow in a vise, hooking a spring scale to the string, and drawing it 28 inches away from the back of the bow, we get from the scale the amount of pull necessary to draw a standard English arrow to the head.

ARROWS—

The arrows used on a bow are of course of great importance in flight shots. The average native arrow is a crude contrivance and is illy calculated to fly far or straight. Some, such as certain of the Yaqui ones, are of the most primitive types, being heavy, unfeathered, crooked, and rough in the extreme. These are doubtless most effective at short distances where accuracy of flight is not a desideratum.

The best type of arrow which has come under my observation is undoubtedly that made by Ishi, the California Yahi Indian. In flight shooting we have tried several hundred arrows of various kinds, including some of the best English make. Two shafts made by Ishi of bamboo, having a birch fore-shaft and very low-cropped feathers, have repeatedly proved themselves the best flyers. They will carry 10 per cent farther than the best English flight arrow, and 20 per cent farther than the standard target arrow weighing 435 grains. These bamboo flight arrows, therefore, have been used in all our tests (see pl. 10). One is 29 inches in length, the other 25 inches. The former weighs 310 grains, the latter 200 grains. They are feathered with soft turkey feathers, clipped as close as is compatible with steering requirements.

It is safe to say that the average archer cannot draw more than a 29-inch arrow. Even the historical clothyard shaft was a Flemish yard, or only 27½ inches, and was the usual length arrow. The anatomical construction of man renders him incapable of exerting his greatest strength when the extended left arm and the flexed right arm are separated a greater distance than this— 29 to 30 inches. He simply cannot draw the string of a powerful bow past his cheek. This limit is well within 30 inches. That it is possible to draw a weak or even a moderately strong bow over 30 inches, even up to 36 inches, will be shown later.

The average Indian bow, however, is obviously constructed to draw less than 28 inches. This fact, and a study of their arrows and the bending capacity of their bows, will convince any archer that 25 or 26 inches is the average draw of most natives. Wherever possible, therefore, we shot the longer arrows on the tested bows, drawing them till a sense of resistance warned of impending fracture of the bow, then released. In the very short bows we shot only the short arrow. All bows were shot repeatedly, at least six times, over the same ground on calm days. The distance was measured with a tape and marked off into ten-yard sections.

FLIGHT SHOOTING—

The attempt in every test was to get out of the bow all the cast that was in it. No implement was spared out of respect for its age or apparent infirmity.

The methods of shooting were of two types. Mr. Compton shot with a Sioux release: all fingers and thumb on the string, the nock of the arrow steadied between the thumb and forefinger, the arrow discharged from the left of the bow. This would be classified by Morse as a tertiary type. I shot with the English release, or Mediterranean type. There was no apparent difference in the cast of the bows dependent upon these conditions.

The elevation at which each arrow was projected was approximately 45° from the horizontal. A quick release was given each upon full draw. This insures greatest velocity. The bow arm was held very rigidly, and in some instances a forward thrust was given with the bow arm at the moment of discharging the arrow, though no apparent gain accrued from this act. In measuring the flight, the greatest distance was recorded as the full capacity of each bow.

The bows tested are listed below in the order in which they appear in plates 2 to 9.

BOWS

BOWS CHIEFLY FROM THE UNIVERSITY OF CALIFORNIA—

Igorot bow (pl. 2, fig. 1). A simple stave of split bamboo; cross-section a flat parallelogram. It is straight when unstrung; the convex or bark side is the back of the bow. The length is 61½ inches; diameters: at center, 1⅛ by ⅜, circumferance, 3 inches; at mid-limb, 1 by ⅜, circumference, 2⅝ inches; at nock, ⅞ by ⅜, circumference, 2⅜ inches. It has bilateral nocks, simple cuts in the wood 1 inch from the ends. It balances at the center, has no wrapping at handgrip or elsewhere; shows signs of use. The wood is in good preservation. The string is made of three strands of manila fiber with a left-hand rope twist, has a slip knot at the top, and a series of half-hitches with 12 inches of excess string at the bottom nock. It has a soft draw and bends in a symmetrical arc. It jars a little in the hand, is flabby in the cast, but is easy to shoot. It pulls 26 pounds with an arrow drawn 28 inches and shoots 100 yards.

Mohave bow (pl. 2, fig. 2). A simple stave of willow, having a permanent bent position following the string; has stubby bilateral nocks. Length, 67 inches; diameter: at center, 1⅜ by 1 inch, circumference, 4 inches; at mid-limb, 1⅛ by ¾, circumference, 3½ inches; at nock, ¾ by ½, circumference, 2½ inches. A cross-section is a rough quadrilateral. The string is of sinew, two strands, with a left-hand twist, bound permanently with many wrappings and half-hitches at the nocks.

The distance between the string and the center of the bow is 4½ inches. It balances in the center. There is some thin inner bark left on the back; the wood is either stained a dark color or has been smoked. There are no wrappings or decorations on it. It shows signs of use and is in good condition. It has a weak draw and a flabby cast, and jars in the hand. Shooting a 28-inch arrow, it pulls 40 pounds, and has a cast of 110 yards.

Paraguay bow (pl. 2, fig. 3). A heavy, crooked bow, apparently of ironwood; follows the string badly; is almost oval on cross-section; its limbs are tapered sharply, terminating in no appreciable nocks; only a slight shoulder at the upper end; shows signs of much use, is burnished at the center by handling; shows old dry blood stains; has a heavy rope for a string, 3/16 inch in diameter, apparently hemp or commercial clothesline. This string is fastened by a slipknot at one nock and bound with wrappings and half-hitches at the other, with 2 feet excess string wrapped about the upper limb. The distance between the string and the center of bow is 5 inches. Apparently it is kept permanently braced or strung. Length, 71 inches; diameters: at handle, 1¼ by 1, circumference, 3¾ inches; at mid-limb, 1½ by ⅞, circumference, 3¼ inches; near nock, 9/16 by ⅜, circumference, 1¾ inches.

It is a stubborn, strong, inflexible, quick-casting bow; very unpleasant to shoot, twisting in the hand and kicking when released. It has a 25-inch draw, past which it refuses to bend; it pulls or weighs 60 pounds, and has a cast of 170 yards.

Because the wood of this bow seemed so resilient, an experiment was undertaken to improve its cast. By heating the wood the lateral deviations were straightened. The wood was planed off the limbs so that a gradual taper was attained, and the bend was distributed throughout the limb instead of being limited to the extreme ends. Its length was reduced to 5 feet 7 inches, horn nocks of the English type put on, and a linen string applied. The altered weapon became an excellent bow, bending with a fine symmetrical curve, quick in its action and very powerful.

As it stands now, when drawn 28 inches, the bow pulls 85 pounds and casts the Ishi flight arrow 265 yards. With a specially made bamboo flight arrow, a lighter replica of Ishi's but having greatly reduced feathers, this bow shot a flight of 276 yards. This demonstrates what intelligence can do in the bowyer's art.

English longbow, hunting type (pl. 2, fig. 4). Property of S. T. Pope. Made of Oregon yew; spliced in the center; woollen braid handgrip; aluminum nocks; is straight and true and follows the string slightly when unbraced. Thin layer of sapwood left at back; cross-section almost semicircular on the belly and flat on the back. Well balanced, even draw, resilient cast, no kick in hand. String made of 65 strands of Irish linen, number 12, waxed and shellacked; served with silk at nocking point, reinforced with linen, spliced in loops, and covered with kid at nocks. Length of bow, nock to nock, 5 feet 8 inches; diameters: at handle, 1¼ by 1⅛, circumference, 4 inches; at mid-limb, 1⅛ by ⅞, circumference, 3½ inches; at nock, ⅝ by ⅝, circumference 2 inches. When drawn 28 inches it pulls 75 pounds and casts 250 yards. This is a typical old English longbow and will be referred to later in the tests.

Athabascan bow, from near Fort Yukon (pl. 2, fig. 5). A straight, stiff bow apparently of Canadian birch, having two lateral nocks ½ inch from each end. The cross-section is a flat oval. There is a piece of wood lashed to the bow below its center, which stands perpendicularly to the belly and is 3 inches long by 1 inch wide and ½ inch thick. This acts as a rest for the string and prevents it from coming in contact with the belly of the bow. Length of bow, 68 inches; diameters: at handle, 1½ by 1, circumference, 4 inches; at mid-limb, 1⅜ by ¾, circumference, 3½ inches; and below the nocks, 1 by ½, circumference, 2¾ inches. The string is made of three strands of sinews with a right-hand twist and is very rough, finished with a slipknot at the top and by half-hitches below. When braced the string stands 3 inches from the bow and gives a high-pitched musical note. There is no binding at the handgrip and the bow shows evidence of use. In action it is very brash, harsh, and stubborn, twists in the hand when fully drawn, is quick of cast, and very unpleasant to shoot. When drawn 25 inches it pulls 60 pounds and gives a cast of 125 yards.

Luiseño bow (pl. 2, fig. 6). A simple stave of willow, apparently a rabbit bow, with red bands of paint running around it. It shows signs of use. The top of the painted handle is 1 inch above the center. It has short bilateral nocks and is warped out of a straight line, permanently bent, and follows a string badly. It has a two-strand sinew string with a left-hand twist. The upper loop is a fast bowknot; the lower is fastened by half-hitches, and the string is ⅛ of an inch in diameter. Total length of the bow, 55½ inches; diameters: at handle, 1½ by ¾, circumference, 3½ inches; at mid-limb, 1½ by ⅝, circumference, 3¼ inches; below the nocks, 1 by 2, circumference, 2½ inches. On cross-section this bow is a flattened oval. It is very soft on the draw, jarring in the recoil, weak in the cast, and is a very poor weapon. When drawn 26 inches it weighs 48 pounds and casts 120 yards.

12 A STUDY OF BOWS AND ARROWS

Navaho bow (pl. 3, fig. 7). A well make bow of mesquite wood, backed with sinew, having a buckskin handgrip 5½ inches in width and sinew wrappings at the tips, running 6 inches down from the nocks. Total length, 44 inches; diameters: at handle, 1 by ¾, circumference, 3 inches; at mid-limb, ⅞ by ⅝, circumference, 2⅝ inches; below the nocks, ½ by ½, circumference, 2 inches. On cross-section it is convex on the back and flattened on the belly, with the bark side toward the back. The string is two strands of twisted sinew, left twist, ⅛ of an inch in diameter, having a fixed loop at the upper nock and half-hitches at the lower, where a buckskin lash terminates the string. The bow is fairly straight along the back but follows the string when unbraced. This bow shows good workmanship, is stiff and quick in action, with no jarring in the hand. The handgrip is practically in the center of the bow and the limbs bend equally. The string gives a good musical hum and is 4½ inches from the bow when strung. The weapon shows signs of use. When pulled to 26 inches it weighs 45 pounds and shoots 150 yards.

Yurok bow (pl. 3, fig. 8). A flat sinew-backed bow, very well made of a good grade of yew wood, apparently from a limb; sapwood shows on the edges. Thick sinew covers the back and extends up over the nocks which are bent in a reverse position. A circular band of sinew runs about each nock 1 inch back of the extremity of the bow. When unstrung this bow is markedly reflexed and has a handgrip of spirally wound buckskin thong. The handgrip itself is 4½ inches wide. Length of bow, 54 inches; diameters: at handle, 1⅞ by ½, circumference, 4 inches; at mid-limb, 2½ by ⅜, circumference, 5 inches; below the nocks, 1 by ⅜, circumference, 2 inches. On cross-section it is a very flat ellipse. The string is composed of two strands of sinew, is ⅛ of an inch in diameter, and fixed at the upper limb by a permanent loop and at the lower by half-hitches. In action this bow is soft, springy, bends in the hand, is flabby in cast, and kicks. When drawn 28 inches it weighs 30 pounds and casts 140 yards.

Alaskan bow, probably Eskimo (pl. 3, fig. 9). A well made, powerful bow of the elementary composite type. The wood is Douglas fir, a square-cut, straight-grained piece such as we commonly see in a building joist. It is backed with a strip of bone 22 inches long, ¼ inch wide, and ¼ inch thick. This is lashed in position with twisted sinew arranged in an ingenious network, constituting a continuous backing from nock to nock, with circular bindings about the limbs at intervals of an inch. On cross-section the wood is flat on the back with beveled flat sloping surfaces on the belly. Length, 56 inches; diameters: at handgrip, 1½ by ¾, circumference 5 inches; at nock 1 by ⅝, circumference, 3¼ inches. It has short bilateral nocks, a thick sinew composed of many twisted strands, and served loops at the ends. The upper end of the string has an extension loop to keep it in position when the bow is unbraced. There is serving of some weed-like material on the string at the center.

This is the first aboriginal bowstring under our observation that has any serving at the nocking point of the arrow. The whole bow is by far the best made of any aboriginal weapon in the group. It is well balanced, rigid in its draw, is exceedingly strong, and has a musical twang to the plucked string. The action is sharp and there is no kick in the hand. When drawn 26 inches it weighs 80 pounds and shoots 180 yards. It seemed such a good bow in spite of the brash quality of the wood employed that Mr. Compton, who was making the test, was urged to draw an arrow the full 28 inches, whereupon the bow fractured at the center with a loud report.

A companion bow to this specimen was repeatedly shot with all sorts of arrows and proved to be a wonderfully good weapon for short-distance, forceful shooting. It is no doubt a most effective implement for hunting big game at close range, say up to 60 yards.

When not braced the bow is practically straight; when braced, with the string the set length found on the bow, the distance between the string and the handle is only 4 inches. This is what archers would term a low-strung bow. By twisting the string before bracing it this distance could be increased to 5 inches, the usual distance in aboriginal bows.

A low-strung bow is better for hunting because it strains the bow less during the long hours of anticipation. High-strung bows have a cleaner cast of the arrow and produce less strain on the string, but greater fatigue to the bow.

Yaqui bow (pl. 3, fig. 10). This is a much used bow, of Osage orange or *bois d'arc*. It seems to have been made by splitting a limb; there are many knots on the bark side, which constitutes the back. These knots are raised, no attempt at leveling them having been made. On cross-section it is rather wide and flat, having the natural curve of the wood for the back and a flat surface for the belly. The bow follows the string. Length, 59½ inches; diameters: at handle, 1½ by ⅞, circumference, 4 inches; at mid-limb, 1¼ by ⅝, circumference, 3⅜ inches; at nock, 1 by ⅜, circumference, 2⅜ inches. There are short pin nocks with wide, square shoulders. The string is one-strand twisted rawhide, 3/16 of an inch in diameter, with a slipknot at the top and half-hitches at the bottom, where the string tapers off with a buckskin thong. When braced it stands 5 inches from the handle. A dull hum comes from the plucked cord. It is a strong, useful bow, jars little in the hand, very resistant at the last of the draw, but a pleasant bow to shoot. It seems, like the preceding weapon, to have been made for strong effective shooting. When drawn 28 inches it pulls 70 pounds and casts the flight arrow 210 yards. This is the best distance made by any aboriginal bow in our tests, and speaks well for the wood employed and the art of the bow maker.

Yana bow (pl. 3, fig. 11[2]). A red yew stave having all the sapwood removed; backed with thin rawhide and having a rawhide handgrip. Its general shape is flat and wide, on cross-section it is lenticular, slightly flatter on the belly side. The nocks are short pins with square shoulders, the last inch of the limb being bound with sinew. The bow is straight; slightly recurved at the extremities of the limbs. It is a good specimen of Ishi's work. Total length, 55 inches, considerably longer than was his custom to make bows; diameters: at handle, $1\frac{5}{8}$ by $\frac{5}{8}$, circumference, 4 inches; at mid-limb, $\frac{3}{4}$ by $\frac{1}{2}$, circumference, 4 inches; below the nock, $\frac{3}{4}$ by $\frac{3}{8}$, circumference, $2\frac{1}{4}$ inches. The string is of twisted sinew, $\frac{1}{8}$ inch in diameter, having a formed loop at the top, and bound with half-hitches at the lower nock. A cotton loop runs from the upper end of the nock and serves to keep the string in place when not braced. The distance between string and bow when braced is $4\frac{1}{2}$ inches.

This bow when drawn 26 inches, the usual draw of the Yana Indian who made it, pulls 42 pounds. When drawn 28 inches it pulls 48 pounds and shoots the Ishi flight

---

[2] Made by Ishi in 1915. Property of S. T. Pope.

arrow 205 yards. This seems to be an adequate strength for hunting purposes, since we know that Ishi killed bear and deer with a similar bow.

Blackfoot bow (pl. 3, fig. 12). A red painted bow, probably of ash. It has no backing. One limb is badly sprung and has a lateral cast. The bow is slightly reflexed in the handle. It follows the string, has a left lateral nock at the upper end, and a right lateral nock at the lower. On cross-section it is a rounded quadrilateral. As no string accompanied the weapon a light linen string was supplied.

Length, 47½ inches; diameters: at handle, 1⅜ by ¾ inches, circumference, 3⅜ inches; at mid-limb, 1¼ by 9/16, circumference, 3 inches; at nock, ¾ by ⅜, circumference, 2 inches. When braced 4 inches it is harsh and unpleasant to shoot, and twists in the hand. When drawn 25 inches it pulls 45 pounds and shoots 145 yards.

If this is the type of a Plains Indian hunting bow, that bow was a poor one.

JESSOP BOWS

Through the courtesy of Mr. Joseph Jessop, of Santa Barbara, California, I was able to test a series of bows in his large collection. He was requested to send a number of his strongest and best preserved American Indian bows, and graciously supplied the following:

Apache bow (pl. 4, fig. 13). A well-made bow, having the classic cupid shape. The wood seems to be white hickory whose straight grain suggests that it was made from a wagon hoop. It is backed with sinew and has a narrow binding of the same at the center. Length over all, 41 inches; diameters: at handgrip, 1⅝ inches, circumference, 3 inches; at mid-limb, ⅞ by ½, circumference, 2¾ inches; at nock, ⅝ by ⅜, circumference, 2 inches. It is flat on the belly and back, and on cross-section it is quadrilateral. There are short bilateral nocks. The limbs are decorated on the belly by figures in red stain. The string is of sinew, two strands twisted, having a slipknot at the top and half-hitches at the lower nock. When strung it proves to be a lively little bow whose weight is 28 pounds when drawn 22 inches, and shoots 120 yards. It did not seem safe to draw this bow any more than this distance; the arrow that accompanied it was only 24 inches long, which indicated that the maximum draw probably had been reached. This is a very nice little bow but apparently meant for killing only rabbits and small game.

Cheyenne bow (pl. 4, fig. 14). A rough, ugly bow made of ash, apparently from the limb of a tree, and heavily backed with sinew. The workmanship is very crude. The bow is straight and thick with a cross-section almost round or a flattened oval at the mid-limbs. There is no binding on it anywhere; the nocks are shallow depressions in the sinew. Length, 45 inches; diameters: below the center, 1¼ by ⅞, circumference, 3½ inches; at mid-limb, 1⅛ by ¾, circumference, 3¼ inches; below nock, ⅞ by ⅝, circumference, 2½ inches.

The string is a rough twist of two strands of sinew, having a slipknot above and half-hitches at the lower nock. When braced and drawn 20 inches it weighs 65 pounds and casts 165 yards. It is a stiff, stubborn bow, very unpleasant to shoot, not made for show, but capable of driving an arrow with considerable force. Probably if drawn 24 inches, which is the limit of the arrow length, it would pull about 80 pounds. It would serve no doubt for killing buffalo and for war purposes. It shows no particular signs of having been used, though it has been greased.

Hupa bow (pl. 4, fig. 15). A typical California Indian bow, made of a good quality of yew, broad and flat in the limbs, heavily backed with sinew, and having nocks formed of overlapping and circular bands of the same material. It is strongly reflexed. The handgrip is of buckskin thong bound about the center. It is painted red and blue in a checkered design over the back. Length, 47 inches; diameters: below handgrip, 1½ by ½ inches, circumference, 3¾ inches; at mid-limb, 2¼ by ⅜, circumference, 4¾ inches; at tips, ⅞ by 7/16, circumference 2 inches. The string is very smoothly twisted sinew resembling a 'cello string, having a formed loop at the top, and made fast at the lower nock by slipknots. A bit of cotton string extends from the loop to the upper nock. When braced this bow is very musical, has a soft, even draw, and weighs 40 pounds; drawn 22 inches, it shoots 148 yards. In action it bends in the center and consequently kicks in the hand. It would seem to be a good bow for small game.

Osage bow (pl. 4, fig. 16). A rather unusual type of bow. It has a small cylindrical handgrip, wide, flat limbs, and small whip-end tips. It is apparently made of *bois d'arc,* and has no backing. The workmanship is excellent. It is 47½ inches in length, the handle is round and approximately ⅞ of an inch in diameter. Just below this the limb is very broad and has a diameter of 2 by ⅝ inches, circumference, 4½ inches; diameters: at mid-limb, 1½ by ½, circumference, 3¾ inches; at tip, ⅝ by ⅜, circumference, 1½ inches. The string is sinew of the usual type. The nocks are short, shallow, and rounded. When drawn 20 inches it weighs 40 pounds and shoots 92 yards. It is a pleasant bow to shoot, but weak.

A STUDY OF BOWS AND ARROWS 19

Cree bow (pl. 4, fig. 17). A flat lath of ash bound with sinew at the handle and nocks, but having no backing. It is fairly straight 44 inches long. There are short bilateral nocks. Its diameters are: at center, $1 5/8$ by $1/2$, circumference, $3 7/8$ inches; at mid-limb, $1 3/8$ by $7/16$, circumference, $3 3/8$ inches; below nock, 1 by $3/8$, circumference, $2 1/2$ inches. The string is sinew, with a slipknot above and the usual hitches below. This specimen was fractured at the handle when drawn 20 inches, and registered 38 pounds at that moment. It is an inferior type of weapon.

Blackfoot bow (pl. 4, fig. 18). This bow has seen considerable service, and bears evidence of many greasings and hard use. It is a piece of split red hickory, heavily backed with sinew, with short rounded nocks. Length, 40 inches; diameter: below handgrip, $1 3/8$ by $5/8$, circumference, $3 1/4$ inches; at mid-limb, $1 1/4$ by $1/2$, circumference, 3 inches; below nock, $3/4$ by $1/2$, circumference, 2 inches. On cross-section it is lenticular, or a flat oval. The sinew draws it into a reflexed position when not braced. The string is made of two strands of twisted sinew, having a slipknot at the upper nock, and half-hitches at the lower. When braced it is a springy, vigorous weapon, and by far the best shooter in the group. When drawn 20 inches it weighs 40 pounds and shoots 153 yards.

It is possible that in its youth this Blackfoot bow might have been drawn farther and have shot harder, but now it cracks ominously when drawn above 20 inches. This seems to be the type of weapon that was used on horseback and doubtless it is strong enough for buffalo hunting. Mr. Jessop assures me that it is a buffalo bow. If this be the case we must assume that it does not take a very powerful weapon to kill bison.

BOWS FROM THE AMERICAN MUSEUM OF NATURAL HISTORY—

Professor A. L. Kroeber was instrumental in obtaining a number of bows from the American Museum of Natural History, New York. They were as follows:

Congo bow (pl. 5, fig. 19). This bow is merely the limb of a tree similar in appearance to our alder. It is split by dehydration, and too brittle to be shot. Length, 52 inches; on cross-section it averages ⅞ inch. It has a sinew of fine vegetable fiber string and conical nocks with slight shoulders. The excess string is bound about the upper limb in a decorative pattern. It is permanently bent, and apparently was kept strung up all the time. In its youth it may have been a fairly good little bow. The workmanship is admirable, but the wood and the size of it prove that it was not a very effective weapon.

African bow (pl. 5, fig. 20). This bow is made of ironwood, is 59 inches long, is reflexed at the handle, crooked, and follows the string. It has conical nocks with a leather ring around the bow at these points to guard the string against slipping. It is ovoid on cross-section. At the handle it is ⅞ by ⅜ inches, circumference, 2¾ inches; at the mid-limb, ⅝ by ⅝, circumference, 2⅜ inches; below the nock, ½ by ½, circumference, 1⅞ inches. There was no string, so one was supplied of waxed linen. When drawn 18 inches, which was apparently all the bow would stand without breaking, it weighed 54 pounds.

Shooting the short flight arrow six successive times, its best cast was 107 yards. A fairly effective weapon at short range, it is an unpleasant bow to shoot, being harsh and tending to twist in the hand.

Andaman Islands bow (pl. 5, fig. 21). Very peculiar in shape, having a small cylindrical handgrip, broad flat limbs, and slender tapering nocks. It is made of a white, fine-grained wood, about the quality of our birch. Total length, 62 inches. At the handle it is 1 by ⅞ inch; at the mid-limb, 2⅝ by ⅜ inches, circumference, 5⅜ inches; ⅜ by ⅜ inch at the nocks. The limbs in cross-section are two flattened arcs; the upper limb is reflexed. Fiber rings encircle the nocks to prevent the string from slipping. There was no string and a linen one was supplied. When drawn 20 inches the weight is 45 pounds; it did not seem safe to draw it farther. Its cast was 142 yards. This is a very fair sort of a bow and shows good workmanship.

South American bow (pl. 5, fig. 22). A black longbow of *palma brava*. It is square in cross-section and has the usual rope string of this type. The excess is bound about the upper limb in a decorative way, which shows that the archer had no conception of what is required of a bow for strong shooting. This dead weight on a limb would interfere with its resilient recoil. Length, 74 inches. At the center the bow is ⅞ by ⅝ inches; at the mid-limb, ¾ by ½ inches; at the nock, which is a slight shoulder, ½ by ⅜ inches. When drawn 28 inches it weighs 50 pounds and shoots 98 yards. Its action is heavy, slow, and jarring. Considering the excellence of the wood, this bow speaks of a lack of intelligence on the part of the maker.

Solomon Islands bow (pl. 5, fig. 23). A heavy, dark, well made bow of *palma brava*. Length, 74 inches; broad in the center, tapering to conical nocks. On cross-section it is lenticular in shape, with a rounded belly but with a wide groove running down the back. At the center it is 1½ by ⅝ inches, circumference 4 inches; at the mid-limb, 1¼ by ⅝, circumference, 3¼ inches; at the nock, ½ by ⅜, circumference, 1¾ inches. The string is of some vegetable fiber, twisted and polished, and is served at the center with thin rattan ribbon for a distance of 4 inches. The string is attached to the nocks in a peculiar way. A loop is made by repeated half-hitches, applied in a reversed manner, every alternate cast. This is stuck together by some adhesive substance, thus forming a permanent cap of matted string for a loop which covers the nock for a distance of an inch or more. It is a very well made string. This bow weighs 56 pounds when drawn 26 inches and shoots 148 yards. Possibly it could have been drawn farther, but I doubt that its cast would exceed 175 yards under any conditions. Although it bends in the handle and in consequence jars the hand, it is nevertheless a good effective weapon.

New Guinea bow (pl. 5, fig. 24). A well-made bow 71 inches long, broad and flat on the back. On cross-section it shows a low arc. It is made apparently of *palma brava* and is bound at the conical nocks and at the middle of the lower limb with rattan sewing. The string is a flat bamboo ribbon. There is no handgrip. The bow shows signs of having been greased. At the center it is 1⅝ by ⅝ inches, circumference, 4 inches; at the midlimb, 1⅜ by ½, circumference, 3½ inches; at the nock, ⅝ by ⅜, circumference, 1½ inches. This bow was not in perfect condition so it was deemed inadvisable to risk weighing or shooting it.

Philippine bow, probably Mindanao (pl. 5, fig. 25). Made of split bamboo, bark left on the belly of the bow; rattan binding at the handgrip. The string is a ribbon of split bamboo, with formed loops and rattan sewing at the ends. There are posterior nocks; two near together at the upper extremity. Length, 55 inches; flat, weak, and of no apparent value as a weapon. The second nock at the upper end apparently was used to make the bow higher strung when desired. It was in no condition to be shot, but probably was no stronger than the one described in the previous group. Its cast would not exceed 100 yards.

African bow (pl. 5, fig. 26). Practically the same as that described as a Congo bow. It was not shot, being apparently too brittle.

TARTAR BOWS—

Tartar bows (pl. 6). My brother, Major B. H. Pope, U. S. Army, stationed in the Philippines, went upon an extended hunting trip into China. His journey carried him beyond the Chinese Wall into the province of Shansi and the Gobi Desert. At my request he obtained two Chinese bows from this location. The Chinese donor of these specimens had practiced archery when a boy. He offered the Major several bows from which the two strongest were selected, with a number of Chinese arrows.

The weaker of these bows was designated as a number three bow, and apparently meant only for target practice. It is in perfect condition although supposed to have been made in the Ming dynasty or over a century ago. It is of course composite in structure and strongly reflexed. The belly is composed of whalebone or horn of the water buffalo inlaid on the edges with some yellow metal. The handle is of shagreen, or shark skin. The back is covered with a thin veneer of birch bark. The ears or ends of the limbs are of a wood resembling beech. The nocks are of inserted buffalo horn. The string is silk, terminating at each end in a long loop. The knot of the loop is a perfect bowline knot, and serves as a resting place for the string as it crosses the bone fulcrum or block which all these Asiatic bows have on their upper and lower limbs. This fulcrum serves to keep the string from slipping when the bow is braced, and likewise gives a clean vibration of the string when the bow is discharged. The string is served its entire length with silk thread and has special serving at the nocking point. There are decorations at the handle. Altogether it is a beautifully made weapon. Entire length, 74 inches. Just above the cylindrical handle it is 1 by 1 inch, circumference, 3¼ inches; at the mid-limb, 1½ wide by ¾ thick, circumference, 3½ inches; at the beginning of the ear it is 1⅝ by ½, circumference, 3½ inches. The cross-section of this portion of the bow is a double flat arc. The ear itself is quadrilateral and measures ¾ by ¾ inches. The bow weighs 1½ pounds avoirdupois, and pulls 30 pounds when drawn 28 inches. It shoots the Chinese target arrow which accompanies it 90 yards, and the Ishi flight arrow 100 yards. It is possible to draw this bow very much farther than 28 inches, because it is so flexible and weak. I therefore drew the Chinese target arrow back some 36 inches, and it flew 112 yards.

The larger of these Chinese bows is truly a huge affair and seems to have been constructed for some giant in strength. It is composite in type, composed, like the other, of horn, wood, and probably sinew, although this cannot be seen because of the covering of birch bark.

These Chinese from whom the bow was obtained said that the entire structure was covered with the gut of a pig. There is no evidence to prove this, and certainly the horn is not covered but shows many cracks from drying and age. The birch bark is perforated at many places by numerous minute holes where some tropical insect has eaten its way into the wood. This bow had been kept in a Chinese temple in the town of Guei-hua-chen; it was an old war bow of the last dynasty, and is probably over 100 years old. Before using the weapon I anointed it repeatedly with raw linseed oil to prevent it from breaking. Length, 74 inches over all. From nock to ear it is 9 inches. The handgrip is made of a piece of pigskin, and the bow at this point is 1½ by 1½ inches, circumference, 4¾ inches. At the mid-limb, which is flat and broad, it is 2 by 1, circumference, 5 inches; near the outer wooden limb, 2¼ by ¾, circumference, 5 inches. This outer limb is a 1¼ by ½ inch quadrilateral.

This bow weighs 3¼ pounds and when drawn 28 inches it pulls 98 pounds. The string of the bow is an immense rawhide rope, the size of rope ordinarily used to lassoo cattle. It is composed of many twisted strands, ending in large loops at each end. Here, as in the smaller bow, the loop is tied with a bowline knot, and rests upon a large bone block or fulcrum. This string is 65 inches long from loop to loop, ⅜ inch thick, and 6 ounces in weight. The bow is so strong that it is necessary to place the handle in a bench vise and call upon another man to assist in bracing it. When braced no white man could pull it. My brother asserts that the Chinese who gave him the bow not only could string it himself but could shoot it. Neither Mr. Compton nor I could pull the string back more than one foot, so we resorted to a method of strapping the bow to our feet and while lying on our backs pulling the string with two hands. By this means we were able to shoot the weapon. It could be drawn up over 30 inches this way, and apparently lost none of its casting power in the maneuver.

The war arrow which came with the bow is a huge shaft 38 inches long with an iron head 4 inches in length (pl. 12, fig. 1). Its diameter is ½ inch and its weight is 4 ounces. Drawing this arrow 30 inches, it flew only 100 yards.

A special bamboo flight arrow 37 inches long was constructed, having a bone nock and made expressly large to fit the string. Its weight was 1½ ounces. It shot 110 yards when drawn 36 inches. The Ishi flight arrow, drawn 29 inches, shot only 90 yards.

The poor showing of this bow was a great disappointment, because we expected a long flight from it. Tartar bows are supposed to be capable of shooting a quarter of a mile. There seemed to be no structural deficiency in the implement, but its cast was slow, dull, jarring, and impotent considering the great amount of force necessary to draw it. Part of this lubberly action seemed to be due to the excessively heavy string. I therefore constructed a string of 90 strands of Barbour's number 12 Irish linen, well waxed and twisted, and having strong hemp loops for the nocks. It weighed 2 ounces and had a diameter at the center of $9/16$ of an inch. With this string the bow cast the war arrow 105 yards, the bamboo flight arrow, 161 yards, and the Ishi flight arrow, 175 yards. Many other arrows were tried on this bow, all with the same disappointing results. Evidently, at least for light arrows, a heavy string may seriously impede the cast of a bow. (See below under An Experiment in Bow Strings.)

That none of the failure of this bow to come up to our expectations might be due to our method of shooting it with our feet, we tried shooting the English longbow for comparison, drawing it with two hands and the feet. Its cast was 250 yards, or practically the same cast as when shot in the proper way, showing no loss of cast ascribed to this change of release.

This Tartar bow exemplifies two things: first, that the excessive leverage of the inflexible end limbs is no advantage, but rather detracts from the resiliency of the bow, and throws most of the work of the bow up near the handle where it does little good; second, that apparently the Chinese conception of warfare entailed the use of dreadful appearances and intimidation, and that these principles applied to bows do not make them more efficient engines of destruction. They shot mighty bows and enormous arrows, which more nearly resembled javelins, but these were so impotent when compared with the robust, effective shooting of the English longbow, or the Turkish composite bow, that the Chinese suffer by comparison, as they must have suffered in martial contest.

JAPANESE BOWS—

A Japanese archer, Mr. H. Shimizu, of San Francisco, gave me the opportunity to shoot one of his target bows (pl. 7). It was the usual composite, reflexed bow of his people. Its length was approximately 7 feet 4 inches and it measured approximately 1 inch square at the handgrip, which is situated at some distance below the center. It seems that the Japanese gauge the strength of their bows by the diameter at the handle. The cross-section of a limb is practically quadrilateral.

The bow under trial was of medium strength. It weighed 48 pounds when drawn 28 inches though it was capable of being drawn 34 inches or more. It cast the Japanese target arrow that was employed by Mr. Shimizu, drawn to its full length—32 inches—a distance of 156 yards. Ishi's flight arrow, drawn 29 inches, made a distance of 182 yards. Mr. Shimizu was not able to better these distances. He had several weaker bows, weighing about 35 pounds, which were not tried for their cast. I was unable to obtain a strong Japanese military bow. Doubtless it is an excellent weapon.

Mr. Shimizu gave me a short section of a bow which he had sawed in two. It was composed of five pieces of wood, the three in the center being respectively mulberry, bamboo, mulberry, while the belly and back were thin strips of bamboo. These were glued together and bound at intervals with rattan or bamboo ribbon.

The string was most excellently made of twisted hemp fiber, sized with some sort of glue or starch, and served at the loops with red silk ribbons. Although about 1/8 of an inch in diameter, which is the size of an English bow string, this Japanese string was not strong enough to stand the strain of a 50-pound English longbow, but promptly broke when used.

The Japanese target arrows are of bamboo, 34 inches in length, 3/8 in diameter, nicely feathered with fish hawk feathers, and have a very true flight. The nock is an inserted plug of some hard white wood resembling boxwood, while the pile or point is a short conical iron cap. Their weight is 448 grains.

NEGRITO BOW—

Mr. R. F. Barton gave me an opportunity to shoot a Negrito bow (pl. 8), a specimen from his Philippine collection. It was a well made weapon of *palma brava*, 6 feet 4 inches in length, excellently finished, having a rounded back and a concave belly, making a most unusual cross-section. At the center it is 1 by 3/4 inches, circumference, 3 1/8 inches; at the mid-limb, 7/8 by 5/8, circumference, 2 3/4 inches; at the nock, 1/2 by 3/8, circumference, 1 3/4 inches. It has short conical nocks with slight shoulders. The string is twisted and highly polished vegetable fiber, having no well formed loop. This string broke during the tests, and a linen string was substituted. When drawn

28 inches it weighed 56 pounds. It cast its own arrow, a long bamboo shaft, a distance of 124 yards. The Ishi flight arrow was shot 176 yards. It is of fairly good wood but follows the string badly, is heavy in the hand, and kicks. *Palma brava* is very much inferior to yew, cedar, or hickory.

POLYNESIAN BOW—

A Polynesian bow, made of some heavy black wood, was given me by Mr. John Wightman, a South Sea Island merchant. Length, 6 feet 7 inches. Its general shape is flat on the back and convex on the belly, wide in the center, with tapering ends. There are conical nocks with carving on the outer limbs just below them. Center, $1\frac{3}{4}$ by $\frac{5}{8}$ inches, circumference, $4\frac{1}{8}$ inches; mid-limb, $1\frac{1}{4}$ by $\frac{5}{8}$, circumference, $3\frac{1}{8}$ inches; at the nocks, $\frac{1}{2}$ by $\frac{1}{2}$, circumference, 2 inches. No string was attached, and a linen one was supplied. When drawn 28 inches it weighs 48 pounds and casts 163 yards. Its cast is sluggish and heavy and it jars in the hand badly. It is not a good bow from an archer's standpoint. With a longer flight arrow, and drawing it over 34 inches, this bow shot 187 yards.

The arrows that came with the bow, two in number, were of bamboo, 5 feet long, with a heavy black wood for a foreshaft and no feathers. They were apparently intended for shooting fish. When shot over the target course they flew most erratically and their extreme range was 136 yards. These arrows were beautifully decorated with engraved formal designs, bound at the nocks and joint with foreshaft, with a dark fiber-like rattan.

REPLICAS OF ANCIENT BOWS—

In an effort to obtain a Turkish composite bow for trial I visited the supply depot of Mr. Francis Bannerman, of New York, a dealer in antique arms. He had several Turkish bows, but all were in such a stage of disintegration that they were incapable of being used. I therefore constructed (pl. 9, figs. 1 and 2) a composite bow of cow's horn sawn in strips ½ inch wide and 12 to 14 inches long, glued on a base of hickory 4 feet long, ¼ inch thick, and 1¼ inches wide, which had been previously bent by heat into a strongly reflexed curve. On the back of this hickory were laid one hundred strands of number 3 surgical catgut and a strip of thin rawhide. The whole form was carefully rasped into shape and encased in thin rawhide, bound at intervals with linen thread. The general plan of the bow followed the description of the Egyptian composite bow found in a tomb at Thebes supposed to be of the time of Rameses II. This specimen has been carefully described by Dr. von Luschan.[3] I also took into consideration the dissection of a Persian bow detailed by Mr. Balfour.[4] My completed product was a very powerful and well made bow, representing excellently this type of implement. Length, 48 inches, the width of the mid-limbs 1¼, the thickness ¾ of an inch. A cross-section is oval. The string is of linen, 90 strands Barbour's number 12. This bow weighs 85 pounds when drawn 29 inches.

With this bow I hoped to exceed the American flight record of 290 yards made by Maxson in 1891. But so far the best flight from it has been 9 yards less than the record and was made under unusual circumstances. The

---

[3] See Badminton, p. 63.

[4] See Structure and Affinities of the Composite Bow.

bow was shot both with the Ishi arrow, which it cast 250 yards, and a 25-inch bamboo flight arrow, shot through a 5-inch *papier mâché* horn. By this latter device it was able to shoot 266 yards; but with an especially light bamboo arrow 30 inches long, having a birch foreshaft, tipped with the jacket of a 30 calibre army rifle bullet, the shaft being feathered with very minute soft owl feathers, I was able to shoot 274 yards. Upon one occasion when the string broke at the moment of recoil, the arrow flew 281 yards, which is the farthest shot ever made in our experience on level ground.[5]

The "Mary Rose" bow. It is a strange circumstance that with all the wealth of material in the line of archery tackle which existed in England up to the seventeenth century, there should be preserved not one single specimen of the English longbow or arrow. One hears of the marvelous deeds of English archers of old and the strength of their artillery, yet we have no specimens of this fleeting glory to view in reverence. The only real link between romance and reality lies in the existence of two unfinished staves found in the sunken vessel, "Mary Rose." This English ship went down off the coast of Albion in the year 1545. She was recovered in 1841. There were on board, besides matters of no interest to archery, two yew staves in good preservation which measure 6 feet 4¾ inches, with a girth of 4½ inches; in the mid-limb the circumference is 4 inches, and 1 foot from the tips the circumference is 3¼ inches.[6] There were no nocks on these bows and no handgrip. Because of their age they have never been bent, weighed, or shot.

---

[5] Shooting a 68-pound yew bow and a bamboo flight arrow with the wind slightly in my favor, and the ground falling on a gentle slope, I once shot 300 yards and 8 inches.

[6] See Badminton, p. 124.

32   A STUDY OF BOWS AND ARROWS

Their strength has been variously estimated from 75 to 100 pounds.

In order to have some reasonable data on the subject of the famous English longbow, I undertook the construction of a replica of these bows (pl. 9, figs. 3 and 4). I selected a very fine grade of Oregon yew seasoned five years, red and clear grained, running 40 lines to the inch; there was ⅜ of an inch of white sapwood. Of this yew I made a bow the exact dimensions of the "Mary Rose" longbow. The finished stave had a formidable appearance, and to look at it, one would say that it was a very powerful weapon, probably pulling over 85 pounds, and must have a correspondingly long cast.

It was shot with simple wooden nocks and a linen string of 75 strands. When drawn 28 inches it weighed only 52 pounds and shot the flight arrow 185 yards. This undoubtedly is due to the great length of limb, which gives added leverage. When drawn 36 inches it weighed 72 pounds and shot the long bamboo flight arrow 212 yards. When drawn 36 inches it shot the replica of an old English broadhead or war arrow, described later, a distance of 117 yards. These records are another distinct disappointment and seemingly are not the fault of the quality of the wood in the bow or of its construction.

To test whether or not this bow might not improve in cast were it made shorter, it was cut down to a length of 6 feet. It weighed now 62 pounds and shot the Ishi flight arrow 227 yards. We know of course from Toxophilus[7] that the standard English bow was cut down from

---

[7] Ascham-Toxophilus, p. 109: "Take your bow into the field, shoot in him, sink him with dead heavy shafts, look where he cometh most, provide for that place betimes, lest it pinch, and so fret: When you have thus shot in him, and perceive good shooting wood in him, you must have him again to a good cunning and trusty workman, which shall cut him shorter, and pike him, and dress him fitter, make him come round compass everywhere, and whipping at the ends, but with discretion, etc. . . . . ."

these stock lengths to suit the size and strength of the archer who shot them. The average bow was the height of a man and his arrow three-quarters of the standard yard, or about 28 inches.

This bow was again cut down to a length of 5 feet, 8 inches between nocks. The limbs were tapered a trifle to distribute the strain evenly over the short arc thus formed. The weapon under these conditions weighs 70 pounds when drawn 28 inches and shoots the flight arrow 245 yards, thus showing the advantage of a properly adjusted stave. Since there is a great difference in the casting quality of wood, it is possible that another stave may have made a stronger bow.

Cliff dweller's bow. The oldest aboriginal American bow (pl. 8), that came under our observation is one obtained from the cliff dwellings of Arizona. The circumstances of its discovery are unknown. It probably represents a type of bow used in pre-Columbian times and possibly is over one thousand years old. The workmanship on this bow is excellent. It is a juniper stave 4 feet 9½ inches long, slightly reflexed at the handle. It shows signs of long usage and is chafed at the left, above the handgrip, where the arrow crossed it in passage. It is bound at the center with a buckskin thong and apparently is padded slightly with red woodpecker feathers. At the upper and lower edges of the handgrip these feathers project a short distance beyond the binding. At short intervals, up and down the limbs, there is a narrow sinew binding but no evidence of backing.

The nocks are simple truncated cones of a different color than the wood, suggesting that a leather nock or binding kept the string in place. A cross-section of the bow is quadrilateral, slightly rounded on back and belly. At the handgrip, the width is 1 5/16 inches, thickness, 3/4;

at the mid-limb, 1 3/16 by 5/8 inches; at the nock, 1/2 by 3/8 of an inch. Its strength certainly does not exceed 50 pounds. Of course it is impossible to shoot this specimen. It has a recent fracture in the upper limb, suggesting that some one had made some attempt to shoot it. I doubt that such a bow could shoot more than 200 yards. Two arrows (pl. 8) were found with this bow and will be described later.

King Philip's bow. In the Peabody Museum of Harvard University is a specimen of a North American Indian bow[8] which represents the type of weapon used by the natives of New England in the year 1660 A.D. This weapon has been referred to as King Philip's bow. Through Professor Kroeber it was possible to obtain an outline drawing[9] of this specimen and exact measurements.

There is no string and no backing on the bow. It is a simple stave, square in the handle, flat in the limbs, and having small, short, bilateral or shoulder nocks.

Securing a very dense grained, well seasoned red hickory stave, I constructed a bow exactly according to the outline scale and the given dimensions. This replica, when drawn 28 inches, weighs 46 pounds. It shoots the flight arrow 173 yards. It is soft and pleasant to shoot, and could do effective work either as a hunting or war implement. In many ways it resembles the bow of the California Indian with its flat, wide limbs and narrow waist. It would be improved had it reflexed extremities and heavy sinew backing, but the original gives no suggestion of these features.

---

[8] Number 9340.

[9] A note attached to the detail drawing is as follows: "Made of hickory. This bow was taken from an Indian in Ludbury, Massachusetts, in the year 1660, by William Goodenough, who shot the Indian."

AN EXPERIMENT ON BOW STRINGS—

An English bowstring made of sixty strands of Irish linen, Barbour's number 12, weighs three-quarters of an ounce. The diameter, when well waxed, is 1/8 of an inch; length, 5 feet 8 inches. Each strand of thread has a tensile strength of 6 pounds, or the entire string has a breaking point of 360 pounds. A Negrito string made of some compact vegetable fiber, 6 feet long, 1/8 of an inch in diameter, weighs three-quarters of an ounce.

A comparative test of bowstrings was made with strands of linen, silk, and catgut. Pieces of each of these substances, having a universal diameter of 250 microns, averaged the following breaking points:

Linen thread	6 pounds
Silk thread	4½ pounds
Catgut	4 pounds
Cotton thread	3½ pounds

Combining five of these threads into one string gave the following breaking points:

Linen	30 pounds
Silk	24 pounds
Catgut	22 pounds
Cotton	18 pounds

Waxing the threads did not increase their strength. Its use seems to be to keep the fibers from fraying; to reduce the diameter, thus cutting down air friction, and to protect the fibers against moisture.

Catgut soaked in water loses its tensile strength. Catgut of course is only the elastic and fibrous tissues from the submucous coat of sheep intestines. It is identical with the sinew of tendons. Sinew strings do not hold their length under tension, but stretch perceptibly, and are very susceptible to moisture. Cotton stretches under strain. Silk deteriorates when dyed, with age, and when exposed to sunlight. Linen is more durable than silk, and never stretches after it is once put on the bow. It is by far the best material for bow strings. Many substances have been tried to size or stiffen strings, but nothing seems so good as wax having a small proportion of resin.

EXPERIMENTAL DATA ON BOW WOOD—

The question—what constitutes the best material for bows?—has been answered in an empirical way by the usage of thousands of years. Of all known woods, yew is most resilient and elastic. Many other woods, such as hickory, bamboo, and *palma brava,* will stand a great deal of bending without breaking, but their recoil from the bent position is sluggish and weak. Compared with yew wood, spring steel is slow and dead. Experiments have long ago shown that metal is not fit for hand bows, and even on the crossbow it is poor material.

In the use of yew we take advantage of two qualities inherent in its structure. The red or heart wood is resilient and has a great capacity for standing compression strain. This gives the desired recoil from the bent position. The white sapwood has the quality of being tough, resistant to fracture, and of great ductile strength. Its position on the back of the bow serves as a buffer against which the red wood can pull, and prevents fracture, much as a sinew backing would do. The backing of bows with the fascia, tendons, or hide of animals seems to have been an almost universal custom among people using coniferous wood of the temperate or arctic zones.

A STUDY OF BOWS AND ARROWS 37

The famous English longbow, from all the evidence we have at hand, was not backed but was made long for the very purpose of avoiding backing. Having discovered the superior shooting qualities of the unbacked yew, the English attained a higher proficiency in archery than their predecessors. That the early Saxons and Celts did use short backed bows is suggested by a drawing by A. Dürer[10] in which an Irish archer is shown with a bow not over 4 feet long, having recurved ends. The arrows in the picture are about 26 inches long. It is practically impossible to draw any strong unbacked bow to such an arc without fracture. The inference, therefore, is that this bow is backed.

Archers in the past have ascribed the resiliency of their bows to the white or sapwood of the yew. The universal custom has been to place this sapwood at the back of the bow and have it constitute about one-quarter of the thickness. The grain of the white wood as well as the red is never cut in the process of bow making but is followed with great fidelity. This of course adds to its strength. To test whether the white wood or red wood of yew has the more spring the following experiment was conducted:

Three sticks of well seasoned yew (four years) were cut the following dimensions: $3/8$ by $3/4$ by 14 inches:

No. 1, pure white sapwood.
No. 2, coarse grained yellow yew, 16 lines to the inch.
No. 3, fine grained red yew, 35 lines to the inch.

These were set in a vise so that 12 inches projected. To these ends a spring scale was successively attached and the wood drawn a distance of 4 inches from the perpendicular.

---
[10] Badminton, p. 142.

No. 1 registered 8 pounds.
No. 2 registered 11 pounds.
No. 3 registered 14 pounds.

The fine-grained red yew is evidently strongest. The breaking point of each was tested. Number 1 was drawn 12 inches from the straight line without fracture. In fact, it was capable of bending at right angles, without breaking. Number 2 broke at 6 inches. Number 3, when drawn 5 inches, fractured. The white sapwood is thus shown to be more elastic than brittle. The red wood is brash and strong.

To test the shooting qualities of the white and red yew, two miniature bows were constructed, each 22 inches long and of the same diameters throughout.

No. 1, white sapwood. When drawn 8 inches, it pulled 8 pounds.
No. 2, red yew from the same log. When drawn 8 inches, it pulled 10 pounds.

Shooting a 10-inch arrow, weight $\frac{1}{6}$ of an ounce, drawing each shot only 8 inches:

No. 1 shot a maximum flight of 43 yards.
No. 2 shot a maximum flight of 63 yards.

To test them, under conditions of equal weight, number 2 was reduced by shaving its limbs until it pulled 8 pounds, its outer limbs being given a quicker cast thereby. Shooting the same arrow, it now made a maximum cast of 66 yards, demonstrating the superior casting quality of the red wood over the white when drawing the same weight.

Mr. Will Thompson, the well-known American archer, at one time had a bow constructed of several lamina of white sapwood glued together. He hoped by this means to obtain a bow of unusual cast. It is reported to me by

W. J. Compton, who saw and shot this bow in the workshop of Barnes, the Oregon bow maker, that it was a complete failure as a bow and had a dull, weak cast.

To test the influence of backing on the shooting quality of a bow, the small miniature of red yew was heavily backed with catgut strands and very thin rawhide, set with glue. Before backing, the bow pulled 8 pounds and shot 66 yards. After backing, the bow pulled 10 pounds and shot 63 yards. It therefore appears that the backing does not add to the cast of a bow but probably only prevents it from being broken when overdrawn. As a test, an arrow was drawn 10 inches on it and under these circumstances it shot 85 yards. When drawn 12 inches it fractured straight across the handle.

ARROWS

PENETRATION OF ARROWS—

The question of the penetrating effect of arrows shot from the bows of aboriginal peoples and ancient archers has caused considerable speculation. We all have heard of the wonderful deeds of past heroes with the bow, but very few accurate data are extant. A few of the statements of historians are as follows:

Giraldus Cambrensis, writing in the twelfth century, relates that a Welsh archer, shooting at two men who were fleeing toward a tower for refuge, missed his mark, and that two arrows penetrated right through the oak gate, which was almost a palm in thickness.[11]

In the journal of King Edward VI[12] occurs the following entry:

May 14th, 1550. There mustered before me a hundred archers, two arrows apiece, all of the guard; afterwards shot together, and they shot at an inch Board, which some pierced quite, and stuck on the outer board; divers pierced it quite through with the Heads of their arrows, the boards being very well seasoned timber.

Hansard[13] quotes some Spanish historian, probably DeLery, to the effect that one of the early explorers in Florida, wishing to test the power of the native archery, offered a young Indian captive his liberty if he could shoot an arrow through a coat of mail. The garment was hung on a wicker basket and the Indian, standing 150

---

[11] "Itinerarium Cambriar" quoted in Badminton, p. 430.
[12] Badminton, p. 431.   [13] P. 22.

A STUDY OF BOWS AND ARROWS 41

paces distant, shot a flint-headed reed clean through the armor. A second coat of mail was placed over the first, and the Indian shot an arrow with great force through both. After this the Spaniards held their armor in contempt, and devised a protection of felt or padded cloth which shielded them and their horses much better than chain or steel corselets.

C. J. Longman, the modern English archer, conducted a few experiments with the following results: An English target arrow, 5/16 of an inch in diameter, weighing 1 ounce, made of pine, footed with beefwood and tipped with a conical steel pile an inch long, shot from a 65-pound bow at 7 yards, penetrated an oak board 1 inch in thickness so that its point projected through the wood, or a total depth of 2 inches.

A similar shaft, armed with a long spear-shaped steel point, 5¾ inches in length, ¾ of an inch wide, weighing 1¾ ounces, shot from a 65-pound bow, penetrated 4⅓ pads or 140 sheets of Pettit's field gun penetration pads. Each pad consists of 45 sheets of heavy brown paper. A good penetration for a 14-gauge shotgun charged with powder and shot is 35 sheets.[14]

VELOCITY OF ARROWS—

In trying to standardize the factors which enter into the problem of the velocity of arrows, I first determined a standard velocity by shooting 100 yards, on a calm day, and timing the flight with a shot watch.

Ishi, shooting his 45-pound bow with a 1-ounce hunting arrow, required an elevation of 30°, and the time required for the flight is 3 seconds. Mr. Arthur Young, shooting a 50-pound bow with a 345-grain English target

[14] Badminton, p. 432.

arrow, requires an elevation of 15° and 2⅗ seconds of time. Mr. W. J. Compton, shooting a 65-pound bow with a 345-grain flight arrow, requires 8° elevation and 2⅕ seconds of time, or a velocity of 125 feet per second. Mr. Compton, shooting a 50-pound bow with an English target arrow, at 40 yards, requires approximately 1 second, or a velocity of 120 feet per second. This latter figure seems to be a fair average of an arrow's velocity. Shooting a 75-pound bow with a 310-grain flight arrow at 45 yards, the time is approximately 1 second, or 135 feet per second.

STRIKING FORCE OF ARROWS—

In attempting to determine the striking force of an arrow I utilized one of the measures employed by riflemen in estimating the penetration of bullets, and used as a target a large cake of paraffin $2 \times 12 \times 24$ inches, with a melting point of 54° C. To determine the striking force of an arrow, I discharged at this target arrows of various diameters, weights, and points, and the distance which they penetrated was measured from the extreme point to the face of the paraffin slab. This method was used, first, to ascertain the striking force; secondly, the penetration under varying conditions, such as weight, shape of head, size of feathers.

To establish a control, a birch dowel 3 inches long and ⁵⁄₁₆ of an inch in diameter was loosely set in a hole through a board and held perpendicular on the face of this slab of paraffin. A 10-pound weight was dropped on this blunt dowel, from distances of 1, 2, and 3 feet. A fall of 1 foot drove the blunt pin ½ inch deep in the paraffin. A drop of 2 feet drove it 1 inch deep, and a drop of 3 feet drove it 1½ inches.

The foregoing and all the following experiments were conducted at room temperature of about 30° C. It may therefore be assumed roughly that a bow which drives a $5/16$ inch blunt shaft 1 inch into paraffin under these conditions has a striking force of 20 foot pounds, or approximately 10 pounds for every $1/2$ inch penetration.

To measure the striking force of a 50-pound bow, an arrow made of a $5/16$ inch dowel, having a similar blunt head, and weighing 1 ounce, was shot at this paraffin block at a distance of 10 feet. It penetrated just 1 inch, or had a striking force of 20 foot pounds.

A 75-pound bow, shooting the same arrow from 10 feet, drove it in $1 1/4$ inches, or approximately 25 foot pounds.

This measurement may be taken as the maximum striking force of an arrow from the average English longbow, or the arrow of many Indian hunting bows. It is, of course, insignificant when compared with the striking force of a high powered rifle bullet, that is, 2445 foot pounds and 2700 foot seconds of the U. S. Springfield rifle; and yet, as we shall see later on, the damage done by an arrow may be quite as fatal as that done by a bullet.

To test whether a heavy missile strikes a greater blow than a light one, an arrow weighing $1 1/2$ ounces, having a diameter of $5/16$ inch, blunt at the end, was shot from a 50-pound bow. It penetrated $1 1/8$ inches in the paraffin, or had a striking force of $22 1/2$ foot pounds. Increased weight of missile evidently results in increased penetration. This statement probably holds good only up to certain limits, which it is not necessary to define at present.

A similar arrow weighing $1 1/2$ ounces, having a blunt end $3/8$ inch in diameter, shot from a 50-pound bow, penetrated the paraffin only $7/8$ of an inch.

CHARACTERISTIC FEATURES OF ARROWS—

Having the measurements of the striking force of an arrow, it next is of interest to learn what type of arrow will best penetrate solid matter—which type will do most damage as a weapon of destruction. The features of an arrow that figure in this respect are its weight, its feather, and its point. The weight lies in the length, diameter of the shaft, and the specific gravity of the wood. Experience has shown that the best arrow shafts are about a yard or less in length and from 5/16 to ½ inch in diameter. They must be thick enough to be rigid. Many different woods have been used in their construction. Practically all Indian shafts of the better sort are universally 5/16 in diameter or less, while some of the rougher and more formidable of the war or heavy hunting arrows approximate ½ inch. Yaqui arrows are of this diameter; so are Chinese and old English war arrows. Still, this amount of wood seldom weighs more than two ounces and generally less.

EXPERIMENTS IN RIGIDITY OF ARROWS—

To furnish data on this subject, the following arrows loaned by Joseph Jessop were measured and tested as to rigidity:

Name	Length over all	Weight	Maximum diameter	Rigidity test: pounds pressure upon nock necessary to spring arrow ½ inch out of line
Apache	25 inches	320 grams	¼ inch	5 pounds
Osage	32 inches	320 grams	¼ inch	5 pounds
Cree	29 inches	255 grams	¼ inch	5 pounds
Cheyenne	24 inches	315 grams	11/32 inch	15 pounds
Blackfoot	24 inches	320 grams	11/32 inch	16 pounds
Sioux	20 inches	310 grams	5/16 inch	16 pounds
Tomawata	24 inches	300 grams	5/16 inch	10 pounds

A STUDY OF BOWS AND ARROWS 45

Rigidity is an essential feature of an arrow for the reason that the force of the bowstring exerted upon the nock must be transmitted along its axis in a direct line, without lateral dispersion, if the missile is to obtain maximum momentum.

Aboriginal shafts are universally small straight limbs of shrubs, or reeds, having a concentric laminated cross-section, which is well calculated to stand longitudinal pressure and remain rigid. The woods that were recognizable were: dogwood (*Cornus Nuttallii*); hazel; serviceberry (*Amelanchier alnifolia*); arrow wood (*Pluchea sericea*). Seldom if ever is any attempt made to employ split timber in their manufacture. The better developed methods of arrow making, however, make use of split timber, which is later planed and turned into cylindrical shafts. A test of the rigidity of this type of arrow shaft resulted as follows:

Wood	Length	Diameter	Pressure necessary to spring shaft ½ inch out of straight line
Willow	28 inches	5/16 inch	10 pounds
Red pine	28 inches	5/16 inch	12 pounds
English red deal	28 inches	5/16 inch	14 pounds
Douglas fir	28 inches	5/16 inch	14 pounds
Birch, white	28 inches	5/16 inch	15 pounds
Bamboo	28 inches	5/16 inch	16 pounds
Ash	28 inches	5/16 inch	16 pounds
Red hickory (Thompson hunting arrow)	28 inches	11/32 inch	15 pounds
Maple	28 inches	11/32 inch	18 pounds
Mahogany (Manila)	28 inches	3/8 inch	24 pounds
Hickory (McChesney hunting arrow)	28 inches	3/8 inch	30 pounds
Birch	28 inches	3/8 inch	30 pounds
Douglas fir	28 inches	3/8 inch	32 pounds
Birch, well seasoned	28 inches	3/8 inch	35 pounds
Hickory, fine red grained	28 inches	3/8 inch	40 pounds

ARROW FEATHERS—

The American Indian used a variety of feathers on his arrows. Those preferred seem to be eagle, hawk, buzzard, goose, heron, flicker, woodpecker. The Japanese and Chinese employ a fine grade of feather, apparently a fish hawk, also a goose and pheasant. The arrows of South America have gaily colored feathers of parrots.

Methods of feathering.—Practically all arrows have three feathers. The popular opinion of the uninitiated is that they have but two because the older illustrations showed only this number. It may be stated that the only good arrows that have two feathers are on weather vanes.

The ancient Saxons seem to have used four feathers, according to the findings in the Nydam Galleys.[15] These were bound to the shaft with linen thread saturated with pitch, a method calculated to stand water. Ancient flight arrows not infrequently had many feathers attached to them, apparently in the vain belief that a feather lightens an arrow, while in fact it only adds friction to one end.

The process of binding the entire length of the feather by a spiral thread is well illustrated in the picture of the English archer shown in plate 1. Here the thread not only binds the extremities of the feather but runs up the shaft between the barbs and binds the stem fast to the shaft. Silk, saturated with verdigris, seems to have been the popular material for this purpose.

American Indians use sinew, which has a glue content, to bind their feathers, but no attempt is made to glue the rib of the feather to the shaft. This unstable condition of the feather permits of greater irregularity in flight.

---

[15] Archers' Register for 1912, p. 241.

A STUDY OF BOWS AND ARROWS

Experience has shown also that the stripped feather, or that whose rib is scraped very thin, is not so good as that which has been carefully cut with a knife. The latter stands up straighter and endures the rough usage.

Kiowa arrows (pl. 11, figs. 1, 2, 3) are typical game or war arrows. It was not a universal custom among Indians to have the heads of the big game arrows lance-shaped with the idea that they could be drawn out better. A barbed head can be forced through in the process of extracting it. These Kiowa arrows when shot fly very poorly after 25 yards, which may be assumed to have been their hunting distance.

The feathers, of course, are simply for air friction, to keep the rear end of the shaft in the line of progress of the point, and to give rotation or stability to the arrow while in flight. This is invariably accomplished by placing three feathers from the same wing on an arrow. Their warped contours act as revolving planes and establish an axial rotation. Some aboriginal arrows have a spiral arrangement of feathers to assist this motion. But this is an unnecessary exaggeration and retards the velocity and striking force of the arrow, as is shown in the following experiment.

Experiment in feather friction.—A 436-grain target arrow with the regulation feathering $2\frac{1}{2}$ inches long cut in a parabolic curve $\frac{1}{2}$ inch high, has a friction area of approximately 1 square inch to each feather, or three feathers on an arrow present a friction surface of 3 square inches. The diameter of the shaft is $\frac{5}{16}$ of an inch, and the head or pile is shown in plate 10, fig. 2, and plate 13, fig. 4. This typical English target arrow, shot from a 50-pound bow at the paraffin block, penetrated the following distances:

At 10 yards, penetration.................... $1\tfrac{3}{16}$ inches
At 20 yards, penetration.................... $1\tfrac{1}{16}$ inches
At 30 yards, penetration.................... 1 inch
At 40 yards, penetration.................... $\tfrac{15}{16}$ inch
At 50 yards, penetration.................... $1\tfrac{4}{16}$ inch

The same shaft feathered with heavy feathers 1 inch wide and 3 inches long, giving a total area of 9 square inches, shot at the paraffin block with the same bow, are the following penetration:

10 yards, penetration....................... $\tfrac{15}{16}$ inch
20 yards, penetration....................... $\tfrac{13}{16}$ inch
30 yards, penetration....................... $1\tfrac{1}{16}$ inch
40 yards, penetration....................... $\tfrac{9}{16}$ inch
50 yards, penetration....................... $\tfrac{7}{16}$ inch

The loss of penetration evidently amounts to almost 50 per cent and is due to the increased air friction with diminished velocity.

These feathers had a perceptible spiral arrangement, and visibly slowed the flight of the arrow to a speed of approximately 110 feet per second. Such arrows are useful for killing small game at short distances, because they are very accurate in their flight and soon lose their speed after striking the ground, grass, or brush, owing to the friction presented to the air. Maurice Thompson has named this type of arrow (pl. 12, fig. 10) a "fluflu" because a Florida Indian friend had a favorite arrow of this sort which made this characteristic sound during flight.[16]

The speed of rotation given an arrow varies according to the size and concavity of the feathers. It is more rapid in target arrows than in heavy shafts, for heavy heads require more feather surface to turn them than do cylindrical points.

---
[16] Witchery of Archery.

It is obvious that to deliver the greatest blow the arrow should strike with its long axis in the line of direct motion. An arrow wavering or tumbling from improper feathering loses in velocity and striking force. An arrow should have air resistance in proper proportion to its weight. Excessive resistance means loss of striking force.

EXPERIMENT IN ARROW ROTATION—

To ascertain the rate of arrow rotation in flight, the following experiment was performed:

Two arrows having similar feathering were joined by a yard of coarse silk thread, so arranged that the revolution of one took up the slack of the thread paid off by the revolution of the second. They were shot at a sand bank simultaneously from the same bow, one above the other, by which means it could be determined how many revolutions each arrow performed.

From a 50-pound bow with English target arrows three revolutions were made in 10 yards and six revolutions in 20 yards. Some arrows failed to make this number and registered only 3½ revolutions to 20 yards.

For two of Ishi's hunting arrows, the highest average at 20 yards was 4½ revolutions from a 50-pound bow. My own heavily feathered hunting arrows from the same bow at 20 yards averaged 4 revolutions.

It may therefore be stated that an English target arrow shot from a 50-pound bow traveling at a rate of 120 feet per second, revolves at a rate of once every 3½ yards, or approximately 12 times per second. It was very apparent in conducting this test, and in shooting in general, that some individual arrows, due to peculiarities or fault of feathering, do not rotate thus rapidly nor evenly, and some not at all.

In testing many aboriginal arrows, the irregularity of their rotation and flight is a striking exposé of the crudity of their construction. Arrows having feathers all from one wing of the bird and properly placed on the shaft always rotate toward the convex side of the feathers. A single feather from the opposite wing may prevent this rotation.

DIFFERENT ARROWHEADS AND THEIR PENETRATION—

The character of the head on an arrow must also influence its penetration. For tests from this standpoint, a series of arrows with different shaped heads was employed. These are shown in plate 13, and may be described as follows:

No. 1, a 28-inch arrow, $5/16$ of an inch in diameter, made of ash; weight, 1 ounce; feathered with standard hunting type of feathers; blunt point; used principally in the paraffin penetration test.

No. 2, a blunt hunting arrow, $3/8$ of an inch in diameter, 28 inches in length; a $1\frac{1}{4}$ inch round headed screw for point; bound with soldered iron wire. A very useful and durable arrow for killing small game.

No. 3, a blunt hunting arrow, 28 inches long, $11/32$ inch in diameter, hickory; weight, $1\frac{1}{3}$ ounces; feathered heavily with balloon-shaped feathers; empty 38 caliber pistol shell for pile.

No. 4, a standard English target arrow; $5/16$ inch diameter; snakewood footing spliced on end; stele of red pine; small balloon target feathers; weight, 5 shillings, or approximately 436 grains.

No. 5, target or roving arrow. Birch dowel, $5/16$ inch diameter; 28 inches long; aluminum nock; small balloon feathers; weight, 1 ounce; conical point, made of a U. S. army Springfield 30 caliber bullet jacket.

No. 6, small bodkin hunting arrow; 5/16 inch diameter; birch dowel; 29 inches long, shaft feathered by Ishi in typical shape; weight, 1¼ ounces; point made of tapered square spike set in a piece of brass tubing. Is copy of small Greek bodkin.

No. 7, heavy bodkin point; shaft has 3/8 inch diameter; 28 inches long; heavy hunting type of feathers; point is a very heavy tempered steel reamer set in steel tubing of 3/8 inch diameter by a shank and rivet. This is almost an exact copy of the old English war bodkin point taken from the drawings made by Hastings.[17] The entire weight of this arrow is 2½ ounces, and it represents the most formidable missile in the group under consideration. The bodkin point was devised to penetrate steel armor, and in England it supplanted the broadhead after protective devices came into general use. Such a heavy shaft can be shot only from the most powerful bows.

Nos. 8 and 9, Ishi arrows; birch shafts 5/16 inch diameter; 30 inches long; feathered hunting style. The points are flaked obsidian 1¾ inches long and ¾ inch wide, set in resin and bound with sinew. Their weight is 420 grains.

No. 10, spear-pointed war arrow. Shaft of 3/8 inch birch; 28 inches long; heavy hunting feathers; point of heavy lance-shaped steel, 2 inches long, 5/8 inch wide, 1/16 inch thick, set in a heavy brass tubing for a socket, with solder. It is built on the lines of Greek and Japanese war arrows. Weight, 2 ounces.

No 11, blunt barbed arrow; called a squirrel arrow; 3/8 inch birch shaft; 28 inches long; hunting feathers; weight, 1½ ounces; point a blunt lance shape with short barbs. An instrument useful in shooting rabbits, squirrels, and game that tend to carry off a shaft. The barbs hold the quarry until the hunter secures it.

---
[17] The British Archer.

No. 12, an Ishi steel head. In all respects the same as Nos. 8 and 9, only having a steel head of his modern adaptation, 1¾ inches long by ¾ inch wide; bound on the shaft with sinew. Weight, 1 ounce.

Nos. 13 and 14, deer arrows, or heavy hunting shafts of my make, of ⅜ inch birch, 28 inches long; hunting feathers; steel heads barbed; 1½ to 3 inches long by 1 to 1¼ inches wide; riveted and soldered in a shaft of steel tubing. They are a counterpart of the English broadhead; weight, 1½ ounces. The head alone weighs as much as half an ounce.

No. 15, a replica of the English war arrow shown in an old painting (pl. 1) in the Museum of Anthropology, San Francisco. The subject is probably St. Sebastian, painted in Italy about the fifteenth century. It represents an English crusader with his longbow and broad-headed arrow. Taking comparative measurements of the picture with the assumption that this archer shot a 6-foot bow, the dimensions of this arrow are as follows: Length of shaft, 35 inches; diameter, ½ inch; length of head, 3½ inches; breadth, 2½ inches; length of feathers, 9 inches; height, 1½ inches. The weight of the copy is 3 ounces, and it probably represents the famous English broad head, a yard long. The weight of the head alone is a trifle over 1 ounce. It seems likely that such miniature javelins actually were shot by exceedingly long-armed and strong men, but as a rule three-quarters of the standard (as referred to in the Fifth Act of Edward IV, chapter 4, as follows) was the average arrow of the times:

Every Englishman, and Irishman dwelling with Englishmen, and speaking English, being between sixteen and sixty years of age, is commanded to provide himself with an English bow of his own length, and one fist mele at least, between the nocks, with twelve shafts of the length of three quarters of the Standard.[18]

No doubt many men tried to shoot arrows far too long for them, even as Ishi made great heavy shafts for show and war purposes that he could not properly discharge from any bow he ever shot. It was probably considered a sign of prowess to shoot a long shaft. This English war arrow is too heavy and cumbersome to shoot from any bow I can command. Even with an 85-pound bow, its flight is only 112 yards. The bow in the picture does not pull over 75 pounds, and being apparently not over 6 feet long, it is incapable of having a 36-inch arrow drawn to the head without breaking.

Waring, the old English bowyer of the eighteenth century, speaking of a 28-inch arrow, said, "A bow full drawn is seven-eighths broken." The English target bow of today invariably will fracture if drawn 30 inches. And it is true that yew, the most resilient and elastic wood in the world, will not stand an arc greater than 120 degrees, and usually is not drawn more than 105 degrees. To draw a yard shaft on a strong 6-foot bow would require an arc of 180 degrees. This is impossible without sinew backing, which the English did not use. Bows 6 feet 6 inches, however, can stand the strain.

These arrows shot from a 50-pound bow at 10 yards, each one being drawn 28 inches and released with equal technique, penetrated the paraffin block as follows:

No. 1, blunt point, penetrated 1 inch.
No. 4, target point, penetrated $1\frac{3}{8}$ inches.
No. 5, conical point, penetrated $1\frac{3}{4}$ inches.
No. 6, small bodkin, penetrated 2 inches.
No. 12, Ishi steel point, penetrated $2\frac{1}{4}$ inches.

[18] Quoted by Hansard on Archery, p. 379.

54   A STUDY OF BOWS AND ARROWS

The heavier arrows shot from a 75-pound bow at 10 yards penetrated the paraffin as follows:

No. 1, blunt	1¼	inches
No. 2, heavy blunt	1⅛	inches
No. 3, blunt point	1⁵⁄₁₆	inches
No. 5, conical point	2¼	inches
No. 7, heavy bodkin	4	inches
No. 10, spear point	3⅛	inches
No. 11, squirrel point	1½	inches
No. 12, Ishi steel head	2¼	inches
No. 13, deer arrow	2½	inches

In order to test their penetration in wood, I shot at a ⅞ inch fir board, green and very hard, using a 75-pound bow, 10 yards distant. No. 3 drove its point halfway through the board and split out a large segment of wood. No. 7, the large bodkin point, repeatedly split the 12 by 24 inch plank, and on being shot at similar boards of greater length, its point went 3 inches through, measured from the proximal face of the board. Shot into a pine block, it penetrated 2 inches; into a eucalyptus tree, it penetrated 3 inches, including the thin bark.

No. 10, spearhead, entered parallel with the grain and penetrated 3⅛ inches (see pl. 15, fig. 3).

No. 13, deer arrow, entering crosswise with the grain, penetrated 1¼ inches (see pl. 15, fig. 2).

No. 3, a blunt point, shot against a piece of dry seasoned redwood (*Sequoia sempervirens*) ⅞ inch thick, penetrated completely through and stuck out a foot beyond. A segment was fractured from the rear surface of the board at the point of exit (see pl. 15, fig. 1).

In no instance did an arrow penetrate, head, shaft, and feathers, through an inch board. Where half-inch pine was shot at, the heavy blunt arrow and the bodkin point both pierced the wood going completely through; the broadhead offers too much friction to do this.

A STUDY OF BOWS AND ARROWS

COMPARATIVE PENETRATION OF STEEL AND OBSIDIAN HEADS

To ascertain which type of arrow is most effective in entering animal tissue, I constructed a box 12 by 12 inches square and 4 inches deep, having open sides. On these sides I tacked tanned deer hide, hair side out. The interior of this box was filled with a bovine liver. Thus we had a structure simulating an animal's flank, hair, and skin externally, with homogenous dense tissue internally, which could be utilized to measure the comparative penetration of arrows with some degree of accuracy. Shooting a 35-pound bow at a distance of 10 yards, the selected arrows penetrated as follows (pl. 13):

Nos. 1, 2, 3, and 4 did not penetrate the first hide, but bounced off.

No. 5, conical point, entered 4 inches, or to the second hide.

No. 6, small bodkin, penetrated 12 inches.

No. 8, obsidian point, penetrated 28 inches.

No. 9, a trifle broader obsidian point, penetrated 30 inches. This experiment was repeated with the same result.

An obsidian point similar to No. 8 penetrated first hide and 4 inches of liver, and broke on the second hide, abruptly stopping with 4 inches penetrated.

No. 11, squirrel, penetrated 4 inches.

No. 12, Ishi steelhead, 2 trials, 21 inches and 18 inches.

No. 00, Ishi steelhead, similar to above, but made extra sharp by filing, penetrated 22 inches.

No. 13, deer arrow, penetrated 14 inches.

Repeating the experiment with a 50-pound bow at 10 yards, the results were as follows:

No. 2, blunt, rebounds.

No. 4, target point, rebounds.

No. 5, conical point, enters 4 inches.

No. 6, small bodkin, enters 25 inches.

No. 9, Ishi obsidian, goes completely through.

No. 11, squirrel, enters 4 inches.

Nos. 13 and 14, deer arrows, go completely through.

No. 15, English war arrow, goes completely through.

A 75-pound bow shoots the heavy bodkin, the deer arrows, and the English war arrow completely through.

From this experiment it is apparent that blunt arrows will not penetrate a yielding elastic body of this sort, though we know from experience in hunting that they do pass through small animals, such as the squirrel, rabbit, and fox, passing through either the abdomen or chest. Here, of course, the bony skeleton stiffens the yielding tissues and favors a puncture. It is also apparent that bodkin points are not effective in penetrating soft animal tissues, but that a cutting edge is necessary, and that the broadhead has greater penetrating properties because it cuts a path that relieves friction on the following shaft.

The most striking phenomenon is the great superiority of the obsidian point in cutting animal tissue. Arrows Nos. 8, 9, and 12 are identical in weight, feathering, and size of head, yet the steelheads, even when sharpened to a keen cutting edge, do not approach the penetration of the obsidian by 25 per cent. Doubtless the better cutting qualities of glass, combined with the concoidal edge of the obsidian point, give this superiority. The same principle is used in modern bread knives and roller bandage knives; here a rough wavy edge cuts better than does a straight sharp edge.

PENETRATION OF THE BODKIN POINT—

To test the ability of the heavy bodkin pointed arrow to penetrate armor, I discharged it from a 75-pound bow at a distance of 10 yards, against a brass plate $\frac{1}{16}$ inch thick, having a piece of pine board at the back. It

A STUDY OF BOWS AND ARROWS 57

entered to the depth of 1½ inches. Without the wood in back it must have gone through to a greater depth. This brass is the thickness of an old Roman bronze breastplate[19] in the Museum of Anthropology.

To test the penetration of arrows in soft yielding substance, half a pound of raw cotton was made into a pad 12 inches square and 1 inch thick, when compressed. This was covered with muslin and fastened to a box composed of white pine ¼ inch thick. Three broadhead arrows of the type of figure 14 of plate 13, were shot at it with a 75-pound bow from a distance of 10 yards. Each arrow penetrated the cotton and went 3 inches beyond the surface of the board. The heavy bodkin pointed arrow went 6 inches through the pad and board, showing that cotton alone would not constitute effective armor.

The same bodkin arrow from the same bow, striking a tempered steel saw blade $\frac{1}{32}$ inch in thickness, split the steel and penetrated the wooden backpiece to a depth of 1 inch. Shooting it against a piece of cold drawn soft steel $\frac{1}{16}$ inch thick, the bodkin point penetrated ½ inch, then because of its high temper broke squarely off at the plate. To test this bodkin point on armor, I selected a suit of chain mail, probably made in Damascus about the sixteenth century. It is composed of interlocking steel links about ½ inch in diameter, the caliber of wire being approximately no. 22 gauge. Each link is welded and connects with four others. Over the chest and back these links are heavier than elsewhere. The entire suit weighs 25 pounds. A form to represent the human chest was constructed of a thin pine box covered with burlap and the shirt hung on this (pl. 17).

At a distance of 7 yards the heavy bodkin arrow (pl. 12, fig. 6), shot from a 75-pound bow, struck the armor

[19] University of California specimen no. 8-2278.

58   A STUDY OF BOWS AND ARROWS

with such force that a shower of sparks flew from it, and the arrow drove through the center of the back, penetrating 8 inches, piercing one side of the shirt and both sides of the box. It is apparent that armor alone is not sufficient protection against an arrow of this sort.[20]

PENETRATION OF HUNTING ARROWS—

As an example of the penetration of the broadhead, the accompanying photograph shows a young buck shot with an arrow of the type of plate 13, figure 14, from a 68-pound bow at a distance of 50 yards (pl. 18, fig. 1). This animal was shot first completely through the abdomen at 65 yards. The arrow severed the abdominal aorta and flew 20 yards beyond, sticking in the ground. The deer bounded about 30 yards, then staggered, and I approached within 50 yards and shot him back of the right shoulder. The arrow ranged forward through the chest, cutting the great vessel of the heart, and made its exit out the opposite shoulder running down the leg six inches, and was only stopped from going completely through by striking the bone in the leg. This animal died in less than two minutes. This deer is one of eight that we have killed with bows in the past four years. Mr. W. J. Compton shot a running buck at 75 yards, killing him with an arrow which traversed the chest and protruded a foot beyond the opposite shoulder.

In securing museum specimens of grizzly bear from Yellowstone Park under a government permit, Mr. Arthur Young and I shot and killed three adult bear and two cubs with the bow and arrow. These bears were wild and were taken at great risk. The largest animal

---

[20] The experiment of shooting a broadhead at this valuable museum specimen did not seem justified. But I doubt that complete penetration could be made with a head of this type.

was an old male, killed by moonlight, the arrow being shot from a blind at 60 yards.

Mr. Young shot an arrow (similar to pl. 13, fig. 14) completely through this bear's chest, severing the vena cava and producing death by hemorrhage. This bear weighed a little over a thousand pounds.

I shot in the heart and killed instantly a charging female grizzly at a distance of 40 yards. The arrow severed two ribs and buried itself in the heart wall, causing a tremendous flooding of the entire chest cavity with blood.

The bear shown in plate 19 was a female that charged while we were taking her cubs. She was shot with five arrows and had her foreleg broken by a rifle shot before being stopped. The photograph shows the arrows penetrating her body. Besides those protruding from her, there is one lying on the ground at her side which had gone completely through her chest, while one not in this picture penetrated her abdomen, severed the portal vein, and flew ten yards beyond her prostrate form.

THE FLIGHT OF ABORIGINAL ARROWS—

In general it may be stated that aboriginal arrows are inferior in make and shooting qualities when compared with those of higher grades of material culture. The specimens commonly found in museums, are, of course, badly out of shape; they are warped, split, loose in their binding of the head and feathers, and generally in need of repair. Even after being put in good condition, they are nevertheless very poor missiles when it comes to accuracy of flight, and in one quiver the individual specimens are of such dissimilar size and weight that no constant technique is possible while shooting them.

Many of the arrows figured in the accompanying plates were shot from their proper bows. The flight was erratic, flirting, and unreliable. No doubt in the hands of the original owner they were discharged in better form. This truth is apparent when an archer attempts to shoot a strange bow. Picking up a Japanese bow and shooting it either by the Japanese method or the English, one is surprised at the inaccuracy of his shooting. The arrows tend to fly widely to one side. I have often shot Ishi's bow and arrow; using his method, drawing the string with the thumb and holding the bow almost horizontal, I found myself very awkward and my shooting ridiculous.

If an archer accustomed to shooting a bow of one strength changes to that of another, he is at once thrown out of form. This is especially apparent in changing from a heavy to a light bow. Here his muscular adjustment is so unbalanced that in using the English type of shooting his arrows fly far to the left.

COMPARISON OF ARROWS—

The California Indian made a better arrow than did the Plains Indian. The Hupa arrows (pl. 11, figs. 5, 6, 7) are of really excellent workmanship. Their balance and proportions mark them for accurate flight up to the limit of their range, say 150 yards. Shooting these with the Hupa bow, they fly in excellent form, and at distances up to 40 yards their impact is sharp and penetrating.

Figure 8 in the same plate is an ingenious bird arrow. At its point it has four small sticks bound with sinew in a square about the foreshaft. This enlarges its striking diameter, so that it increases the marksman's chances of getting his game. The feathers on this specimen are

A STUDY OF BOWS AND ARROWS

arranged in a spiral position, which again shows the good sense of the maker. This arrangement not only serves to rotate the otherwise difficult head and thus promote steadiness in flight, but the increased friction tends to stop the arrow after 10 or 20 yards, so that it is more easily found when shooting in the trees or in the brush.

The Negrito bird arrow shown in plate 8 employs the same principle of spreading the striking point. Here a series of bamboo spikes are arranged concentrically and make a formidable head for hitting birds. The other two arrows shown are typical fish arrows, hence they have no feathers. These shafts shot at distances greater than 10 yards tend to float and dive in most erratic gyrations. The bird arrow flies heavily but straight. None of these can be shot much over 100 yards from the bow shown on the same plate.

COMPARISON OF ARROWS AND BULLETS—

From the experience derived from these and many other hunting episodes, I am convinced that an arrow that enters either the abdominal or chest cavity of a large animal does as much damage as a bullet, and even seems to cause more hemorrhage than most rifle bullets. The tearing and destruction of tissue is greater in the case of the gunshot wound; but the clean bleeding wound of the arrow is quite as effective as a mortal traumatism. Where an arrow strikes muscular tissue, such as a ham or shoulder, it makes a clean, readily healing wound, and does little harm. So on the whole we feel that the bow is a more humane and more sportsmanlike implement for hunting.

CONCLUSIONS

The conclusions derived from these experiments are:

The aboriginal bows are not highly efficient nor well made weapons.

The greatest flight shot achieved by any aboriginal bow at our disposal is 210 yards.

The greatest flight attained by any bow in our experiments was 281 yards. This flight was made by a replica of a Turkish bow.

The flight arrows made by Ishi are superior to all that we tried.

The English longbow is a superior weapon to any other bow tested. The old English broadhead arrow a yard long really existed.

The striking force of a 50-pound bow with a 1-ounce arrow at 10 feet is 20 foot pounds.

The striking force of a 75-pound bow with a 1-ounce arrow is 25 foot pounds.

The velocity of a target arrow from a 50-pound bow is 120 feet per second; from a 75-pound bow, 135 feet per second.

The heavier the arrow, up to a certain limit, the greater the striking force.

The larger the feathers on an arrow, the sooner it loses velocity and striking force.

The red wood of the yew has more cast than the white wood.

A STUDY OF BOWS AND ARROWS

Backing a bow with rawhide does not increase its cast; it only prevents the bow from breaking.

Obsidian arrow points penetrate animal tissue better than steel points the same size.

Linen is stronger and better for bow strings than sinew.

A Tartar bow, though the most powerful to draw, is a failure as a weapon to shoot.

The California Indian makes the best aboriginal arrow of all the specimens examined.

The English target arrow of today is the highest scientific development of the arrow.

A steel broadhead arrow, shot from a strong bow, can pass entirely through a large animal and produce instant death.

A bodkin-pointed arrow, shot from a heavy bow, can penetrate steel mail.

The bow is a more sportsmanlike implement than a gun because it requires more skill and personal strength, and in hunting it places the man and his quarry on a more equal footing. It fosters the preservation of game.

PLATE 1

AN OLD PAINTING OF ST. SEBASTIAN

In the University Museum of Anthropology. There are two figures painted on small wooden doors, probably those of an ancient sacrarium. One figure represents the Saint, bow and arrow in hand, dressed in armor of the fourteenth or fifteenth century, having on his breast the Cross of the Crusaders. The other figure, not shown here, is that of a kneeling monk, possibly in adoration.

The figure of the archer in the painting stands 29½ inches tall, and the string on his bow is 30 inches long. This bears out the old statement that the string on the longbow should be the height of the archer. Under these circumstances the bow when unstrung is three or four inches longer than the string.

Assuming the bow to be six feet, this would make our archer some five feet eight or nine inches, which probably is a good average for his day. The arrow in the picture is 17 inches over all, with a shaft of 15½ inches.

The proportions maintained by the artist seem to be accurate, and the objects are all in one plane, with no distortion through perspective.

Assuming the bow to have been six feet, comparative measurements of the features of the archer's equipment are computed as follows:

The bow is 1⅝ inches thick and has a nock 1½ inches long. Judging from the appearance, this bow does not pull over 80 pounds, probably less. It is of red yew, with the white sapwood clearly showing on the back. It is gracefully made, having slender whip ends to its outer limbs. There are delicate horn nocks, indicated by light blue-gray color, at the ends, but there is no suggestion of a handgrip at the center. The string is thin and white, therefore not sinew, but probably of hemp, linen, or silk. The delicate nocks and whip ends of the bow are not capable of standing a great strain. Having made about a hundred yew bows myself, I venture to assert that this particular weapon is not one of those very powerful implements described by historians, but one well within the command of such a man as is depicted in the painting. His delicate hands portray the scholar rather than the rustic yeoman.

The length of the arrow over all is 38¾ inches. The length of the shaft is 35 inches. Its diameter is a trifle less than half an inch. The length of the head is 3¼ inches, its breadth, 2¼ inches. The feathers are 9 inches long.

The arrow is the famous English broadhead, having a heavy angular steel point set on the shaft with a tubular haft or socket. The whole head seems to have been forged. The arrow is a simple cylindrical shaft of light yellow wood, probably ash or oak. It is tapered slightly at the nock, where there is the suggestion of a long narrow wedge-shaped piece of horn inserted. The feather is the historic gray goose wing, cut straight and angular. It is bound to the shaft at both extremities with white silk thread in close serving. In the interval between these servings, the thread runs spirally up the shaftment, between the barbs of the feathers; the spirals are about a quarter of an inch apart, and fasten the feather through its entire length to the arrow.

A replica of the arrow was constructed to represent as nearly as possible that in the painting, birch being used for the shaft, forged steel for the head, and goose feathers. Its weight is 3 ounces. It is in truth that honorable old institution, the English broadhead arrow, a yard long.

[POPE] PLATE 1

PLATE 2

BOWS USED IN THE TESTS

Fig. 1.—Philippine bow made of bamboo, pulls 26 pounds, and shoots 100 yards. University of California Museum of Anthropology, number 10–587.

Fig. 2.—Mohave bow, pulls 40 pounds and shoots 110 yards. 1–13816.

Fig. 3.—Paraguay bow, made of ironwood, pulls 60 pounds and shoots 170 yards. This specimen was worked over by me into a bow of more scientific proportions, when it then drew a 28-inch arrow, pulled 85 pounds, and shot a flight arrow 276 yards. 16-619.

Fig. 4.—Modern copy of old English longbow, made of Oregon yew, pulls 75 pounds, shoots 250 yards. Property of S. T. Pope.

Fig. 5.—Yukon bow of birch, pulls or weighs 60 pounds, shoots 125 yards. 2–2810.

Fig. 6.—Luiseño bow, pulls 48 pounds, shoots 120 yards. 1–9213.

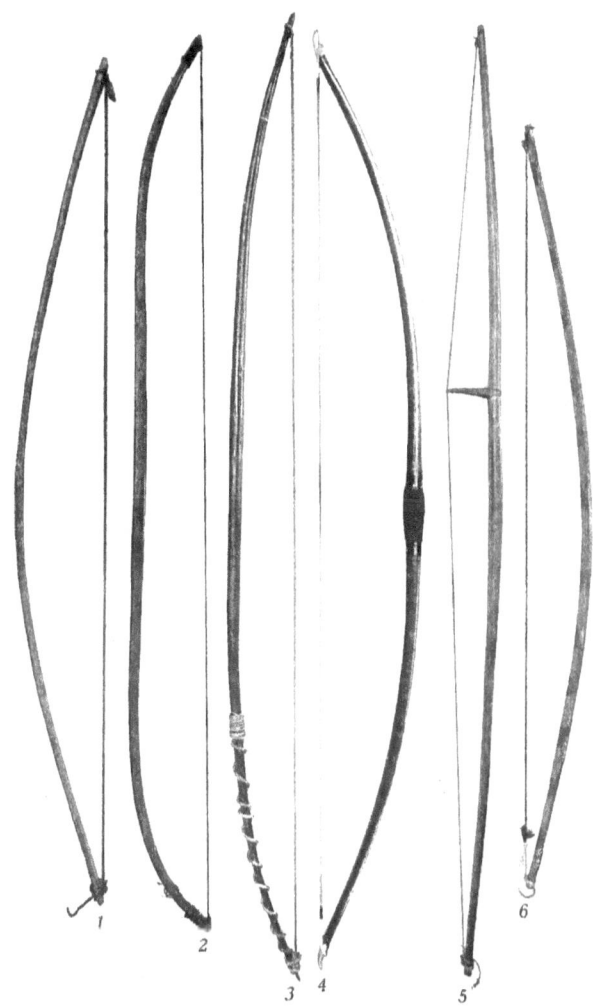

[POPE] PLATE 2

PLATE 3

BOWS USED IN THE TESTS

Fig. 7.—Navaho bow, of mesquite wood backed with sinew, pulls 45 pounds and shoots 150 yards. Museum number 2–5702.

Fig. 8.—Yurok bow, made of yew wood, sinew backed. A typical Northern California specimen. It draws 30 pounds and shoots 140 yards. 1–1055.

Fig. 9.—A powerful Alaskan bow, probably Eskimo, made of fir, backed with bone and open sinew lashing. A weapon suitable for killing big game. It pulls 80 pounds and shoots 180 yards. 2–6372.

Fig. 10.—A Yaqui bow of Osage orange, a rough, strong weapon built for active service. It pulls 70 pounds and casts a flight arrow 210 yards. 3–1875.

Fig. 11.—Ishi's bow. A Yahi specimen, made of yew, backed with rawhide, pulls 48 pounds and shoots 205 yards. Property of S. T. Pope.

Fig. 12.—A buffalo bow, Blackfoot. When drawn 25 inches, the limit of the arrows that accompany it, the weight is 45 pounds and the cast 145 yards. 2–5494.

[POPE] PLATE 3

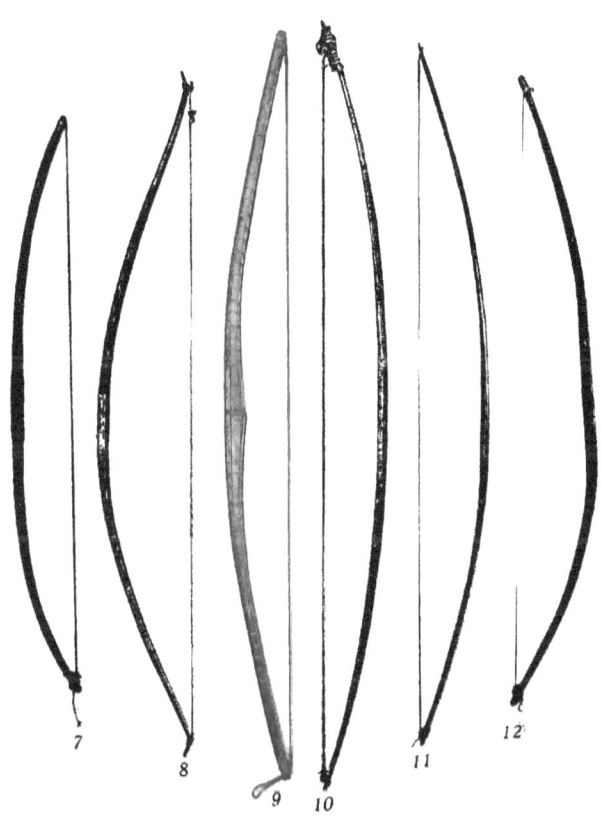

PLATE 4

BOWS AND ARROWS FROM THE JESSOP COLLECTION

Fig. 13.—Apache bow, hickory, backed with sinew. It pulls 28 pounds and shoots 120 yards.

Fig. 14.—Cheyenne, a rough, sinewy-backed buffalo bow, weighs 65 pounds and casts 156 yards.

Fig. 15.—Hupa, a typical California bow made of yew wood, backed with sinew, painted red and blue, pulls 40 pounds and shoots 148 yards.

Fig. 16.—Osage bow, an unusual type made of *bois d'arc*. It pulls 40 pounds and shoots 92 yards.

Fig. 17.—Cree bow, a flat lath of ash which broke while being tested. When drawn 20 inches, it registered 38 pounds and fractured. It would not have cast the flight arrow more than 150 yards.

Fig. 18.—Blackfoot, a hickory buffalo bow, backed with sinew; sprightly little weapon pulling 40 pounds and shooting 153 yards.

The arrows in the plate, from left to right, are as follows: Apache, Cheyenne, Osage, Hupa, Cree, Sioux, Tomawata, Blackfoot.

[POPE] PLATE 4

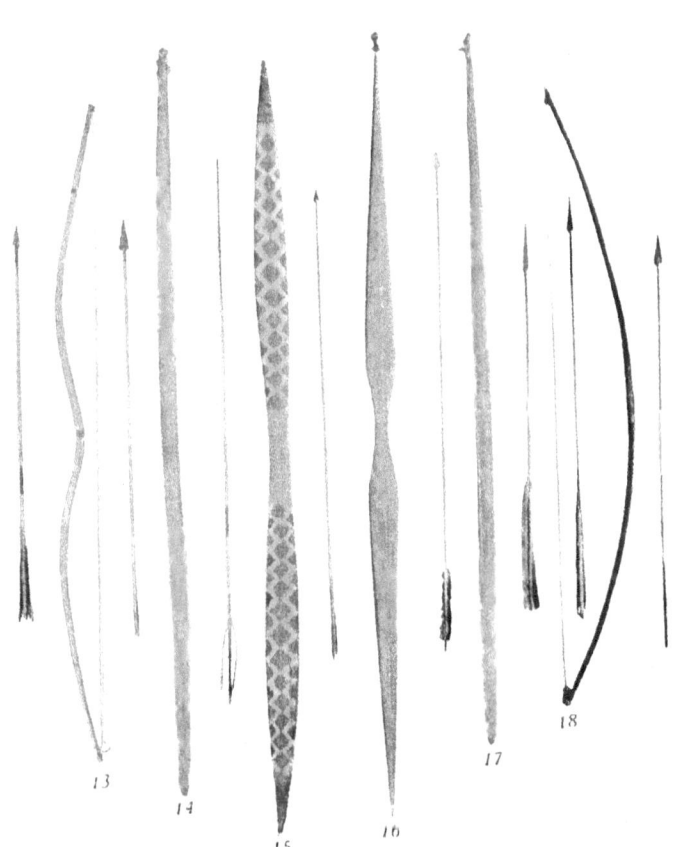

PLATE 5

AMERICAN MUSEUM OF NATURAL HISTORY BOWS

Fig. 19.—Congo, a well-made little bow, but too brittle and cracked to be tested. Specimen number 90-1-3038.

Fig. 20.—African bow, made of so-called ironwood; draws 54 pounds and casts 107 yards. 90-0-280.

Fig. 21.—Andaman Island bow. When drawn 20 inches it pulls 45 pounds and shoots 142 yards. It did not seem advisable to draw it farther. 70-0-1129.

Fig. 22.—South American bow of *palma brava*. When drawn 28 inches it pulls 50 pounds and shoots 98 yards. 40-9800.

Fig. 23.—Solomon Islands, a well-made bow of *palma brava*. When drawn 26 inches it weighs 56 pounds and shoots 148 yards. T. 2669.

Fig. 24.—New Guinea, a well-made bow of *palma brava*, too brittle to be tested. 80-0-3936.

Fig. 25.—Philippine, probably Mindanao, in no condition to be shot; probably does not weigh over 30 pounds nor shoot over 100 yards. Not numbered.

Fig. 26.—Africa, practically the same as fig. 19, and too fragile to be tested. 90-1-182.

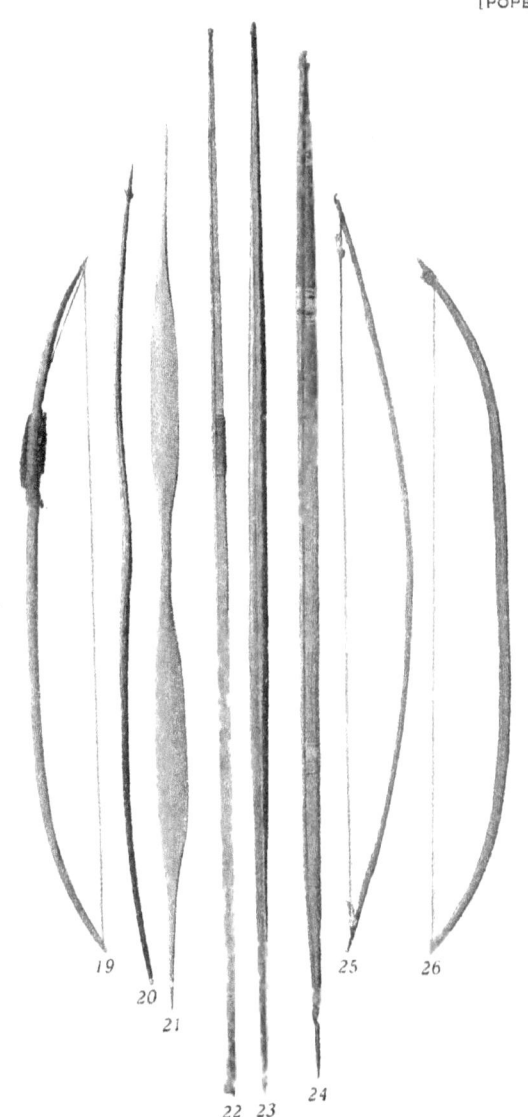

[POPE] PLATE 5

PLATE 6

TARTAR BOWS

Fig. 1.—Tartar bow, number 27, showing the reflexed shape of the composite bow when unstrung, also the long target arrow.

Fig. 2.—The same bow being braced. This weapon, drawn 29 inches, weighs 30 pounds and shoots 100 yards.

Fig. 3.—Tartar bow, number 28. This is the heavy bow, the string of which is like a rawhide lariat. It is a formidable looking weapon.

Fig. 4.—Same Tartar bow being held in position, but no man is able to draw it more than 12 inches. When drawn 30 inches it weighs 98 pounds, and when shot by drawing with both hands and both feet it shoots the flight arrow 90 yards. After change to a lighter bow string it cast the same arrow 175 yards.

[POPE] PLATE 6

PLATE 7

JAPANESE ARCHER AND BOW

Mr. Ogawa in Japanese costume shooting a light bamboo bow, showing the classical attitude. The bow is held "as one holds an egg in his hand"—very lightly. The left forefinger is pointed toward the object to be hit. The arrow is held with the Mongolian release, and drawn on the right side of the bow to the point of the right shoulder. An extra shaft is held in the grasp of the little finger.

Shooting of this sort is part of the high school education in Japan. The distance ordinarily shot is about 30 yards.

This particular bow is 7 feet 4 inches long, is an inch wide and a little less than three-quarters of an inch thick. It pulls about 40 pounds and shoots a target arrow 150 yards.

The Japanese gauge the strength of their bows by the thickness. All are the width of a thumb joint, or one inch. There are three general strengths of bows. One is half an inch thick; the next is three-quarters; and the third, one inch in thickness.

Old Japanese prints and statuary show much shorter and more powerful weapons than that here illustrated.

[POPE] PLATE 7

PLATE 8

NEGRITO, CLIFF DWELLER, AND WINTUN BOWS AND ARROWS

Fig. 1.—Luzon Negrito bow, from the R. F. Barton private collection; made of *palma brava*. When drawn 28 inches it pulls 56 pounds and shoots 176 yards.

The nearest arrow is a bird arrow, from the same tribe. The two other arrows are Melanesian fish arrows without feathers; Museum numbers 11-26, 11-332.

Fig. 2.—Northern Wintun bow and arrows. A reflexed, sinew-backed, yew bow, too fragile to test. At the nocks it is bound with fur, apparently weasel. This device is used to act as a damper to the string so that it makes no noise when the bow is shot. It is said that Geronimo could shoot an arrow with absolute silence. Probably some similar method was employed. Arrows fledged with owl feathers make little or no noise in flight, and although the plumage from this bird seems to have been avoided by the American savage, it is possible that the unholy intent suggested by the necessity of a silent shot in the dark may have warranted such employment. Bow, 2-6813, arrows, 1-4484.

Fig. 3.—Cliff dweller bow from a cave in Colorado. It is probably one of the oldest bows in America. The wood is juniper or cedar. The actual weight is 350 grammes. It probably did not pull more than 50 pounds. 2-3342.

The two arrows found with this bow are made of reed, having a hard wood foreshaft tipped with flint heads. Their weight is 20 grammes or 320 grains. Their general characteristics are those of the Northern California Indian arrows of today. 2-3338, 2-3339.

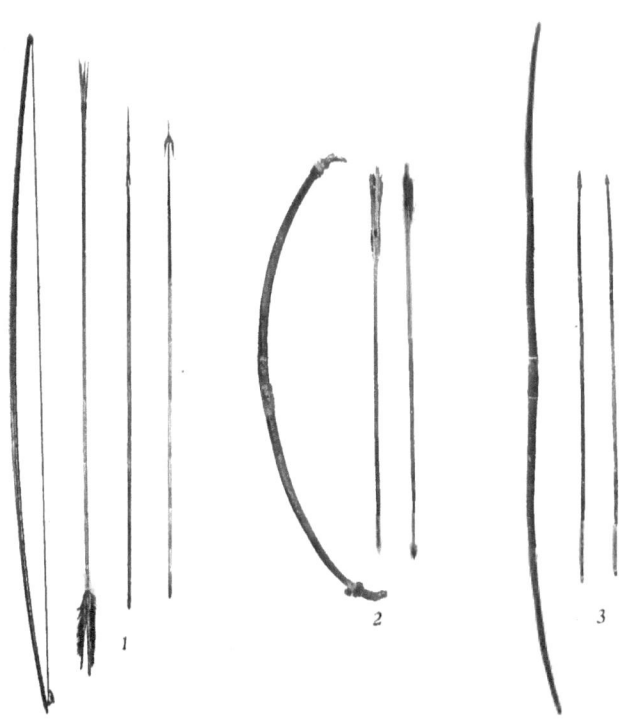

[POPE] PLATE 8

PLATE 9

REPLICAS OF TURKISH COMPOSITE AND ENGLISH BOWS

Fig. 1.—Composite bow unstrung, showing its reflexed condition. The string has been looped on for convenience in handling. The bow thus appears strung, but could of course not be shot until strung with its curvature reversed.

Fig. 2.—Shooting a flight shot with a composite bow. A shorter arrow is shot through a horn. This permits its being drawn past the bow, a method used by the Turks. The weight of this bow is 85 pounds. Its greatest flight is 281 yards.

Fig. 3.—A replica of the "Mary Rose" bow, showing Mr. Arthur Young drawing a 36-inch broadhead arrow on a 6 foot 4 inch bow.

Fig. 4.—The English longbow when drawn to the full arc. Observe symmetry of the curve, showing the even distribution of the strain upon the wood.

The arrow here is drawn to a point on the jaw below the eye, not to the ear as in ancient times. The former has been demonstrated by Horace Ford to be the proper method for accurate aiming. In a man of average height and length of arms, the distance is 28 inches from his extended left hand to his jaw.

PLATE 9

PLATE 10

ARROWS USED IN TESTS

Fig. 1.—One of Ishi's hunting arrows, made at the Museum. It has a birch shaft, steel head, and turkey feathers. It is 30 inches long and weighs about an ounce.

Fig. 2.—The Ishi flight arrow used in all the tests. It is 29 inches over all, made of bamboo, with a birch foreshaft, tipped with a conical steel pile, feathered with turkey feathers and weighs 310 grains. Its flight is uniformly 25 per cent better than the standard English target arrow. Property of S. T. Pope.

Fig 3.—A standard English target arrow of the present day, made of Douglas fir, having a spliced foreshaft of snake wood. It is nocked with horn, has balloon-shaped turkey feathers, is 28 inches long, $5/16$ inch in diameter, cylindrical in shape, and weighs 436 grains or 5 shillings. The end is fitted with a blunt cylindrical steel pile.

Fig. 4.—A bamboo flight arrow, having a birch foreshaft, fashioned after Ishi arrows. Its total length is 25 inches and its weight is 200 grains. The feathers are hawk, but very short and low. It is tipped with a blunt brass pile; shot on small bows.

Figs. 5, 6, and 7.—Arrows made by Ishi while in the wild state. The shaft is made of witch hazel, the foreshaft of some heavier wood. They are feathered with buzzard feathers, bound on with deer sinew, and painted in rings on the shaftment with red and blue pigment. Fig. 7 has a chipped glass head, bound on with sinew. The others have only the notch for such a head. Museum Nos. 1-19577, 1-19578, 1-19579.

Figs. 8 to 13.—Ishi arrows made in the Museum, showing the various sizes and shapes used. The larger seem to have been made more for show or ceremonials or as presents. 1-19864, 1-19863, 1-19866, 1-19862, 1-19456, 1-19454.

[POPE] PLATE 10

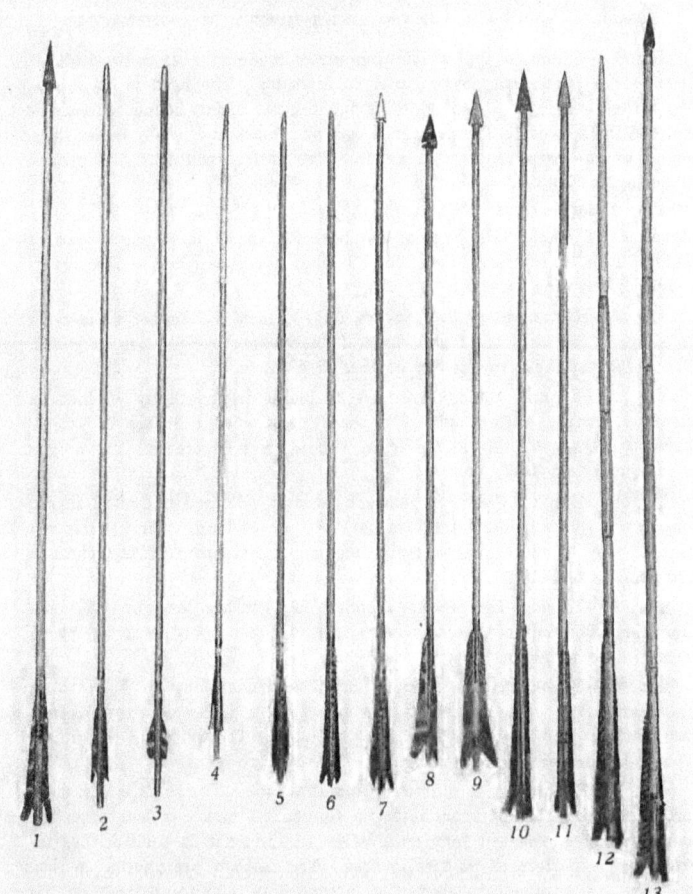

PLATE 11

ABORIGINAL ARROWS IN THE UNIVERSITY MUSEUM OF ANTHROPOLOGY

Fig. 1.—Kiowa, a typical hunting arrow made of a stem or shaft of dogwood 23 inches long by 5/16 inch in diameter. The head is hoop iron, 3½ inches long by ¾ inch wide, having a short shank bound with sinew inserted in the wood. The feather is that of a hawk and is 5½ inches long, bound at the extremities with sinew. The entire weight is 252 grains. Museum No. 2-4831.

Fig. 2.—Kiowa. Shaft possibly dogwood, 21 inches long, ¼ inch in diameter. The head is a piece of flat bone 6¼ inches long, bound in with sinew. The feathers are hawk, sinew bound, 6½ inches long. This arrow weighs 204 grains. 2-4831.

Fig. 3.—Kiowa. Shaft 26½ inches long, ¼ inch in diameter, same wood as above. The head is of thin brass 2 inches long by 5/8 inch in width. The weight of the arrow is 316 grains. 2-4831.

Fig. 4.—Yaqui. Made of a reed 25 inches in length by ½ inch in diameter, having a foreshaft of a heavy dark wood 6 inches in length. There is a sinew binding at the joint. There are no feathers. The weight is 450 grains. 3-1877.

Fig. 5.—Yurok. Shaft of hazel or possibly of "red bud," 29 inches long, by 5/16 inch in diameter; feathers 5½ inches long. The head is red flint, 1½ by ¾ inches, set in resin and bound with sinew. The weight is 320 grains. 1-1448.

Fig. 6.—Hupa. The wood as above, 29¼ inches long by 11/32 inch diameter. The feathers are 4¾ inches in length, head is of bone 2½ by 5/8 inches. The weight is 316 grains. 1-987.

Fig. 7.—Yurok. Shaft possibly hazel, 30 inches long by 5/16 inch in diameter, having a foreshaft of heavier wood 5½ inches long by ¼ inch in diameter. The feather is 7½ inches in length. The weight is 480 grains. This is a blunt arrow for small game. 1-1448.

Fig. 8.—Yokuts. A bird arrow of unusual type. The shaft is 33 inches long by 5/16 inch in diameter, having a foreshaft 7 inches in length, on the end of which are lashed four small cross sticks to act as a head, thus increasing the pattern of its hitting area. The feathers are unusual in that they are cut parabolic in shape and arranged in a spiral manner on the shaft. This not only helps to rotate the inert head, promoting accuracy and stability of flight, but materially slows and shortens the flight, thus making the arrow easier to find after shooting. 1-10767.

[POPE] PLATE 11

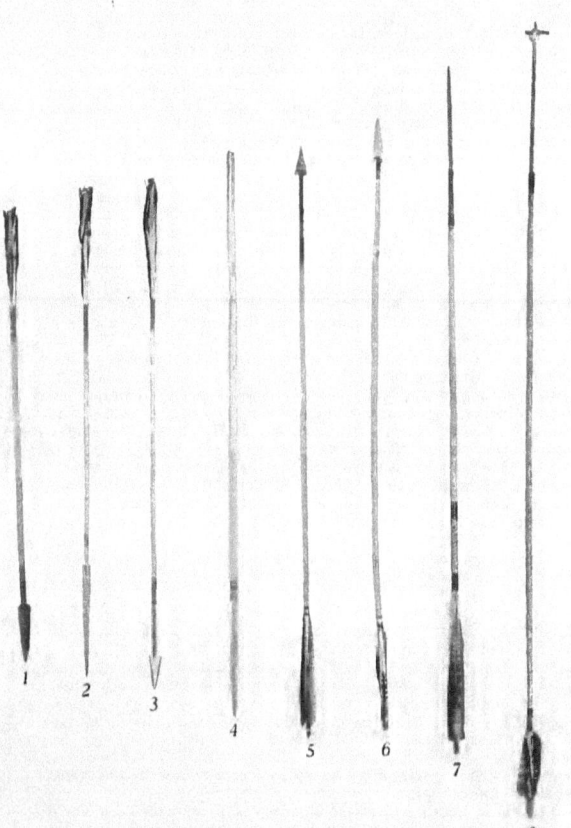

PLATE 12
VARIOUS ARROWS
Property of S. T. Pope

Fig. 1.—Chinese or Tartar war arrow. The shaft is apparently of poplar or beech wood, 38 inches long by ½ inch in diameter. It has a wide oval nock cut in the expanded end of the arrow, and the whole reinforced by a binding of shagreen, or shark skin. The shaftment is stained red, the feathers are goose, 10 inches long, 1 inch high, cut and glued on without binding. The head is of forged iron, 4 inches long, set in the shaft with a shank. The joint is bound with sinew, covered with lacquer. The weight of this missile is 4 ounces. It is the heaviest arrow I have ever seen. Shot from our strongest bow, 85-pound Turkish, its flight is only 115 yards. The arrow really possesses more the qualities and characteristics of a javelin than of an arrow.

Fig. 2.—Chinese arrow, lighter, for hunting or targets. Shaft of wood, similar to above, probably beech, 38 inches long by ⅜ of an inch in diameter, having a simple round nock bound with shagreen. The feather seems to be heron or goose, 13 inches long, cut or scraped very thin on the rib, and glued to the shaft without binding. The point is iron, 2 inches long by ¾ inch wide, set in with a long slender shank. The joint is bound with lacquered sinew. Its weight is 1½ ounces. It can be shot 138 yards.

Fig. 3.—Replica of old English war arrow from painting of St. Sebastian in plate 1. Length 38½ inches, weight 3 ounces. It can be shot 112 yards.

Fig. 4.—Japanese target arrow, a bamboo shaft 35 inches in length by 11/32 inch in diameter. It has a wide hardwood nock about ½ inch long, set on the end, probably with a pin. The joint here is bound with red silk and varnished. The feathers are fish hawk or eagle, the rib cut very thin. They are 6 inches long by ¾ inch high, glued to the shaft, and bound at the extremities with a ribbon of silk floss or paper which is covered with lacquer. Two rings of gold leaf decorate the shaftment. The pile is a short, conical brazed iron cap, set on the end with a pin shank. There is no evidence of shellac or varnish on the shaft. The weight is 432 grains. A very fine arrow. It can be shot 185 yards.

Fig. 5.—Ishi hunting arrow, birch shaft, 30 inches long by 5/16 inch thick, turkey feathers 8 inches long, bound with sinew but not glued to shaft. The head is obsidian set in a notch with resin and bound with sinew. The weight is 485 grains. It can be shot 205 yards.

Fig. 6.—Replica of old English bodkin point, made for piercing armor. The shaft is birch, 28 inches long by ⅜ inch in diameter. The feathers are turkey, 5 inches long by ¾ inch high, cut and glued to shaft; the ends bound with green silk floss. The point is quadrihedral, tapered tool steel, having a hollow shank or haft into which the shaft is set with a cement made of pitch and caoutchouc. The weight is 2½ ounces. With this arrow we were able to shoot through chain mail and steel plate. It can be shot 150 yards.

Fig. 7.—Hunting arrow made by W. H. Thompson, the archer. The shaft is of red split hickory, 28 inches long by 11/32 inch in diameter. It has a simple nock, red dyed turkey feathers, cut in balloon shape 2¾ inches long by ¾ inch high, glued to the shaft; the cock feather is white. The head is made of a lanceolate steel blade, 2 inches long by ¾ inch wide, brazed in a thin tubular socket or haft 1 inch long. It weighs 560 grains. This is a beautifully made arrow proportioned most skilfully. It is the result of 30 years' experience in hunting with the longbow. It can be shot 200 yards.

Fig. 8.—Small bodkin point, fitted to an Ishi arrow, used in the tests. It can be shot 215 yards.

Fig. 9.—Broadhead hunting arrow of old English type, made of a birch dowel ⅜ inch in diameter, 28 inches long, having a tempered steel head 2½ inches long by 1⅛ inches wide, set in steel tubing shaft by rivet and solder. Used for killing big game. Weight, 1½ ounces. It can be shot 190 yards.

Fig. 10.—Blunt arrow for small game, so-called "fluflu," birch shaft, full width cut feathers, screw head bound with wire, weight, 1¼ ounces. It can be shot only 139 yards.

Fig. 11.—Typical English target arrow, length 28 inches, weight, 5 shillings or about 436 grains. It can be shot 235 yards.

[POPE] PLATE 12

PLATE 13

ARROW HEADS USED IN PENETRATION TESTS

Fig. 1.—Blunt headless arrow, used to gauge striking force. Shot against paraffin.

Fig. 2.—Blunt screw head, bound with wire, used for killing small game.

Fig. 3.—Blunt arrow, tipped with empty 38 caliber shell, used to shoot through board.

Fig. 4.—Regulation English target head or pile.

Fig. 5.—Conical head made of empty rifle jacket.

Fig. 6.—Small steel bodkin point used only in tests.

Fig. 7.—Large steel bodkin, replica of old English, used to pierce metal.

Figs. 8 and 9.—Obsidian hunting heads made by Ishi.

Fig. 10.—Lance-shaped head used to pierce armor.

Fig. 11.—Blunt barbed head, set in shaft with a shank, bound with tinned wire and soldered. Used to kill small game.

Fig. 12.—Ishi steel hunting head.

Figs. 13 and 14.—Steel broadheads, used in killing large game. Still longer and broader heads were used by Mr. Arthur Young and myself in killing bears. The blades on the latter were 3 inches long, $1\frac{1}{4}$ inches wide by $\frac{1}{32}$ inch thick. They were made of spring steel, sharpened with a file to a meat-cutting edge. These blades are set in a steel tubing haft, by a rivet and soft solder. They will stand a great deal of hard usage.

Fig. 15.—A replica of the old English broadhead depicted in the painting of St. Sebastian, plate 1. Its length is $3\frac{1}{2}$ inches, width $2\frac{1}{4}$ inches, weight, a trifle over 1 ounce.

[POPE] PLATE 13

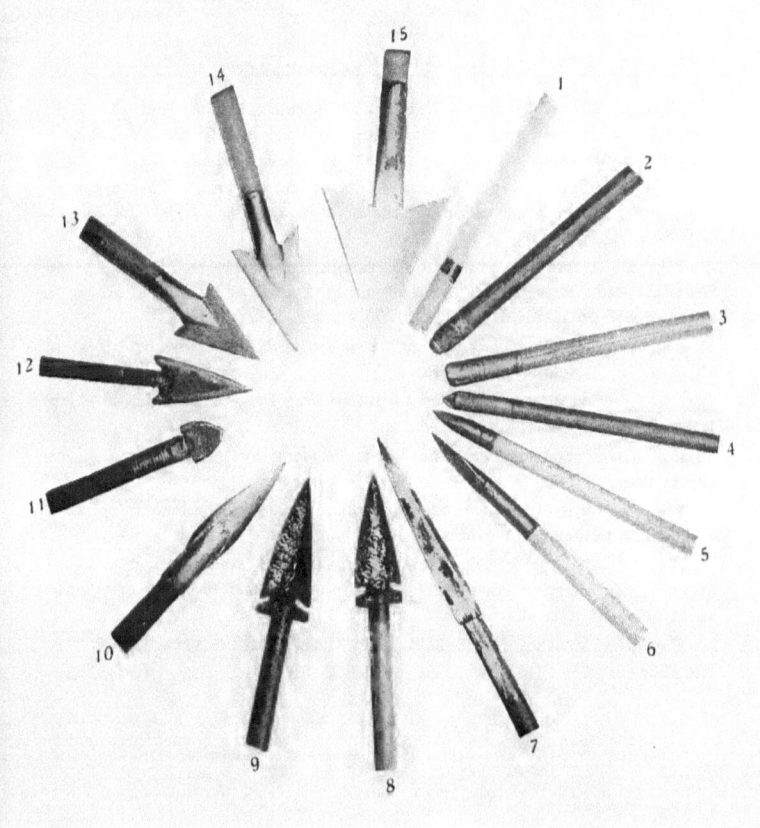

PLATE 14

ANCIENT SYRIAN ARROWHEADS

Figs. 1, 2, and 3.—Small iron bodkin points, showing that the early English had precedence to guide them in fashioning similar heads a thousand years later.

Figs. 4 and 5.—Larger bodkin points of forged iron. The larger of these is a bit over 2 inches long in the blade and $3/8$ inch wide. Its weight is 275 grains.

Fig. 6.—A bronze arrowhead, Etruscan, of classic shape. Its blade restored would measure $1\frac{1}{2}$ inches long by 1 inch wide; the thickness is about $\frac{1}{32}$ of an inch. Its weight is 50 grains.

Fig. 7.—A rounded bodkin point whose length is $1\frac{1}{2}$ inches, width $3/8$ of an inch. The weight is 100 grains.

Fig. 8.—A steel lanceolate head 2 inches long by $5/8$ inch wide, weighing 120 grains. A well-made head.

Fig. 9.—A steel lanceolate head 2 inches long by $3/4$ inch wide, weight 145 grains.

Fig. 10.—A flat bronze head whose blade is $1\frac{1}{2}$ inches long by $3/4$ inch wide. The weight is 85 grains.

Fig. 11.—Though listed as an arrowhead, this seems rather to be a bronze knife blade or lancet. The haft is square and in no way suggests an attachment to a shaft.

Fig. 6 is Museum No. 8–1244. All the others are catalogued under No. 8–231.

[POPE] PLATE 14

PLATE 15

ARROWS PENETRATING A FIR BOARD

Fig. 1.—The penetration of a blunt arrow shot from a 75-pound bow at an inch fir board, showing the type of fracture produced at a distance of 10 yards.

Fig. 2.—The penetration of a broadhead hunting arrow shot from a 75-pound bow at 10 yards. The broadhead has gone in almost crosswise to the grain.

Fig. 3.—A lance-shaped arrowhead shot from the same bow, showing the penetration from a distance of 10 yards.

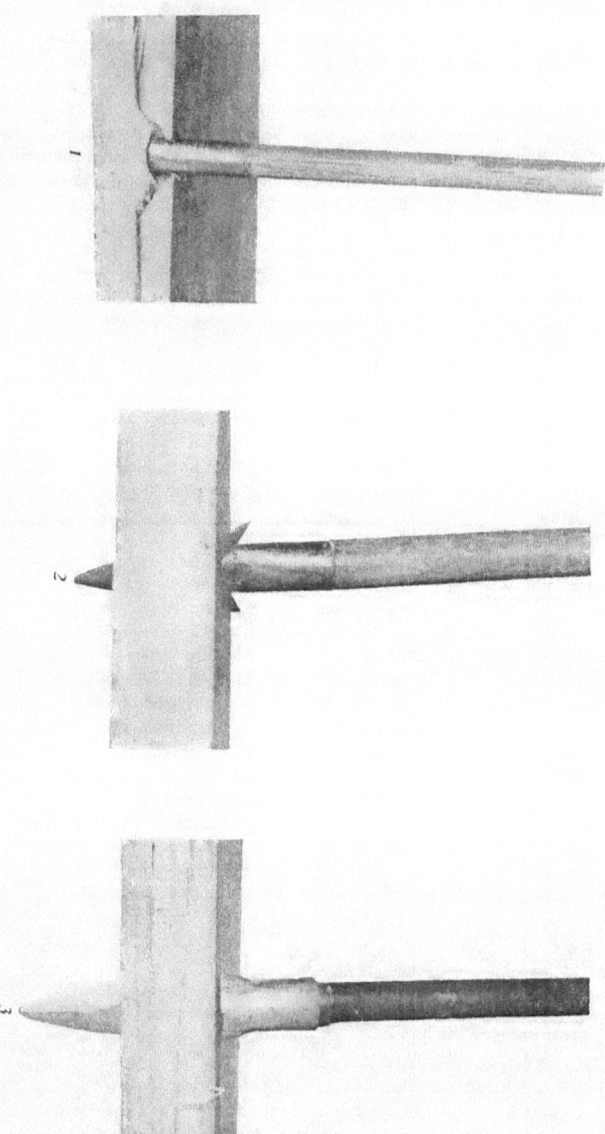

[POPE] PLATE 15

PLATE 16

SKULL PIERCED THROUGH THE ORBIT BY AN ARROW

Fig. 1.—This is the anterior or facial portion of an Indian skull found near Buena Vista lake at the head of the San Joaquin valley, and now No. 12-1731 in the University Museum of Anthropology. It shows certain anomalies of the teeth in that there is a persistent decidual bicuspid in the left superior maxillary bone. The two right upper incisors are missing. The right superior maxilla is fractured and the wall of the antrum depressed inward. The nasal bones are fractured and almost entirely missing. There is a transverse fracture crossing the left superior maxilla cutting the infra-orbital foramen.

Running backward and downward, there is a portion of an arrow shaft about 5 inches in length which pierces the inferior orbital plate, crosses the nasal cavity traversing a portion of the ethnoid, vomer, and sphenoid process, and terminating at a point one inch above the base of the styloid process. This piece of arrow is the major portion of the foreshaft and the spliced joint of the shaft, which is broken off short. The foreshaft is made of some hard wood such as hazel or wild lilac or redbud, while the shaft apparently is of reed. The union between them is formed by a spindle insertion with resin and shows marks of sinew wrapping. The anterior end of the arrow has been burnt off, but the taper indicates that the arrow probably had a stone head attached within an inch of the charred extremity. The apertures through the various plates of bone traversed rather suggest that a small sharp arrowhead passed through. The course of this head passes directly over the foramen spinosum, foramen ovale, and the foramen lacerum medium. It seems therefore that it made its exit posterior to the angle of the jaw about two inches below the mastoid process, on the left. In doing this it must have cut the internal carotid artery and the internal jugular vein. Death must have resulted from hemorrhage within a few minutes.

It may be assumed from the fractured, burned, and punctured condition of this portion of the skull that the individual was a middle-aged Indian who was shot in the eye with an arrow; that he was also struck in the face with a club, thus sustaining a bilateral fracture of the superior maxillae, or that he fell forward and sustained these fractures upon hitting the ground. There are several fractures in the base of the skull which suggest that he may have been beaten on the head and no effort was made to succor him.

The entire absence of calvarium and the burned conditions of the lateral surfaces of the skull, combined with a total immunity from charring both of the face and the part of the bone covered by muscular attachments as well as the preserved arrow shaft, rather suggest that the body lay upon its anterior surface during the burning process and that it was in a state of tissue preservation: burned soon after death.

There has been no attempt to remove the arrow, though the end near the joint is broken, not burned, as if this were done by the victim himself, or by a blow in the face, or in falling. The burning seems hardly such as would be done at ceremonial cremation, more as though the body lay face downward while the hut or the surrounding tules were set on fire.

The arrow must have been discharged at short range, hitting the victim either while he lay on the ground or came forward with his head down in a shielded position.

Fig. 2.—Reconstruction of course of arrow.

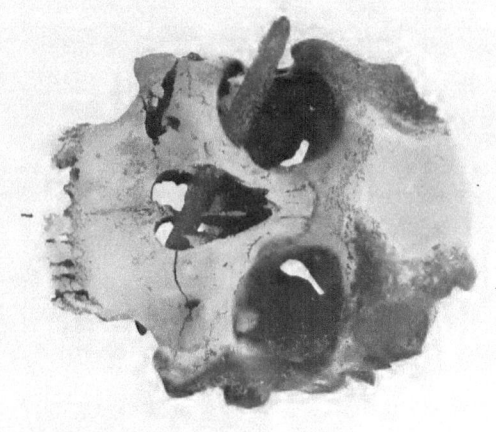

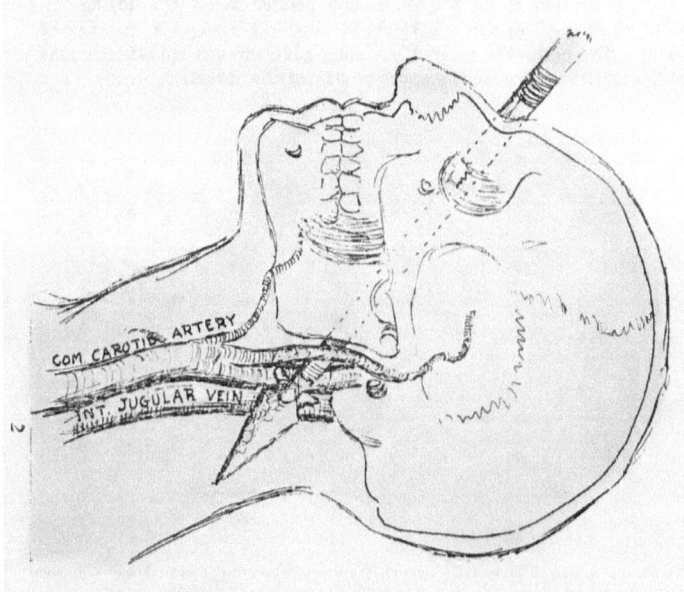

[POPE] PLATE 16

PLATE 17

ARROW SHOT THROUGH A COAT OF MAIL

The penetration of an English bodkin pointed arrow (pl. 13, fig. 7), shot at chain mail armor. A 75-pound bow was used at a distance of 7 yards. The point has pierced one side, gone through a half-inch pine board, and struck against the opposite side of the jacket.

[POPE] PLATE 17

PLATE 18

PENETRATION OF ARROWS

Fig. 1.—The effect of shooting a broadhead arrow (pl. 13, fig. 14), at a deer 65 yards distant. A 68-pound bow was used.

Fig. 2.—Penetration of a redwood board 1 inch thick by a blunt arrow (pl. 13, fig. 2), shot from a 75-pound bow at 20 yards.

[POPE] PLATE 18

PLATE 19

PENETRATION OF ARROWS

Penetration of arrows shot from a 75-pound bow at a grizzly bear 40 yards distant. The story is told in "Forest and Stream," October, 1920.

PLATE 20

PENETRATION OF OBSIDIAN IN BONE

Fig. 1.—Human femur with imbedded obsidian arrowhead which has been snapped across just below the surface of the bone. Found in 1907 in the Ellis Landing shellmound on San Francisco bay. 12-2340.

Fig. 2.—Radiograph of same.

Fig. 3.—Radiograph showing the flat side of the head. The point is driven more than halfway through the bone.

www.ingramcontent.com/pod-product-compliance
Lightning Source LLC
Chambersburg PA
CBHW031124080526
44587CB00011B/1106